JOHN ELDREDGE

AND **LUKE ELDREDGE**

A YEAR WITH MEN

A 12-MONTH PLAN
FOR YOUR GUYS' GROUP

Unless otherwise noted, all Scripture quotations are taken from the Holy Bible, New International Version®, NIV®. Copyright © 1973, 1978, 1984, 2011 by Biblica, Inc.® Used by permission of Zondervan. All rights reserved worldwide. www.zondervan.com. The "NIV" and "New International Version" are trademarks registered in the United States Patent and Trademark Office by Biblica, Inc.®

Scripture quotations marked MSG are taken from THE MESSAGE, copyright © 1993, 2002, 2018 by Eugene H. Peterson. Used by permission of NavPress. All rights reserved. Represented by Tyndale House Publishers, a Division of Tyndale House Ministries.

Scripture quotations marked NLT are taken from the Holy Bible, New Living Translation, copyright ©1996, 2004, 2015 by Tyndale House Foundation. Used by permission of Tyndale House Publishers, a Division of Tyndale House Ministries, Carol Stream, Illinois 60188. All rights reserved.

Band of Brothers® is an original HBO mini-series. © Home Box Office, Inc.

Printed in the United States of America.
ISBN: 978-0-578-32100-4
First Edition

10 9 8 7 6 5 4 3 2 1

CONTENTS

INTRODUCTION

As men, we're meant to live in community.

Few of us ever do.

It's not that we don't want to. It's just unclear how to go about it. That and we've not seen many examples of men doing it well.

That's why we created this guide.

A Year with Men provides a roadmap for focused time with a group of men over the course of a year. While there's flexibility, there's also a plan that lays out what to do, how to do it, when to schedule it, and why it matters.

"No man is an island," John Donne famously said. Those words are so memorable because no matter how deep we dig our moats, we know it to be true. We are not made to live this life and walk this journey by ourselves.

We are made in the image of God, and God exists in perfect fellowship. Long before creation, the Trinity existed in intimate and timeless fellowship. We were created to live in fellowship—in community—as well.

So why aren't more men doing so?

An essential fact about male community is that to have real fellowship, you must have a shared mission. And most small groups lack this component.

Following the rhythms of the masculine soul, *A Year with Men* maps out a season of building masculine community through shared experiences. You'll discover how to know and tell your story—as well as how to respond to the stories of other men. There will be times of rich study and conversation through the *Wild at Heart, Becoming a King,* and *Fathered by God* film series. And there's a guided approach to watching the HBO series *Band of Brothers* together.

But living a year with men is not just about diving into the deep waters of the soul together. It is also about going out and doing, shoulder to shoulder, what feeds the soul.

Through a guided calendar, *A Year with Men* follows an intentional rhythm for weekly gatherings—as well as ideas and ways to pursue off-the-grid adventures with one another. It's an invitation into authentic community that's both life-changing and rare. One that creates space for true fellowship, real healing, and the transformative presence of God.

ROADMAP FOR THE YEAR

Over the course of a year, your group will go through five units—*Wild at Heart*, *We All Have a Story*, *Becoming a King*, *Band of Brothers*, and *Fathered by God*. Each unit has its own introduction, so you don't need to worry about the particulars until you get there.

This is a one-year plan with lots of breaks! In between each unit, we've scheduled weeks for your group to enjoy time together as well as one big group adventure (preferably in the summer).

You can start any time of year—but there are better and worse times to begin. It's ideal to kick things off in January and go through a calendar year. September is another great time to start. On the other hand, May isn't the best time to begin. Most groups take time off during summer so you'll just be getting started when guys will be hitting their summer vacations. The order and content flow will remain the same whenever you start. You'll just need to adjust accordingly for holidays and summer.

For four of the five units, you'll watch a video together and then discuss it through the provided questions. In Unit #2, you'll learn how to tell your story and listen to the stories of the men in your group. Your leader will let you know when there is material to read between weeks. It's also a good idea to always have a journal for any insights or notes.

Healthy groups need room to breathe. After completing Units #1 and #2, we suggest taking a week or two off. Unit #4 is a ten-week study; you'll want a break after that, too. We've built in a week of adventure, but ask your guys what they'd like to do.

We also recommend taking off at least four weeks for summer. This will vary group to group, so talk to your guys about their summer plans but know we've built margin for it into the schedule.

We've intentionally included space for the natural rhythms and interruptions of life. This year-long schedule includes four weeks off *beyond* the scheduled time off—making it 48 rather than 52 total weeks. Use these extra weeks off when you need to. Rather than have a few men missing during summer or holiday seasons, just take a break.

UNIT #1: *Wild at Heart* **Video Series**
Weeks 1-7

Get Out and Do
Week 8

UNIT #2: We All Have a Story
Weeks 9-16

Get Out and Do
Week 17

UNIT #3: *Becoming a King* **Video Series**
Weeks 18-23

Adventure Together
Week 24

Time Off
Weeks 25 - 28

UNIT #4: *Band of Brothers* **Series**
Weeks 29-38

Get Out and Do
Week 39

UNIT #5: *Fathered by God* **Video Series**
Weeks 40-47

Celebrate
Week 48

BEGINNINGS

Let's be honest. Committing to an entire year isn't easy.

How many areas of our lives ask for this level of commitment? An annual lease is a big deal. We set New Year's resolutions but rarely make it past the first month. Even a committed relationship teeters on the underlying assumption that both parties can abandon ship at any time.

Our world has shaped our lives around the short term, around quick satisfaction.

Coffee is getting ever more instant. If we have to wait in the Starbucks drive-through for more than 10 minutes, we grow impatient. Small groups are built around the premise of the six-week study. We get furious when our flight is delayed or, God forbid, *cancelled*. Anything that throws us off our hurried pace is more than irksome. It is tyranny. Anything that challenges our need for speed receives our wrath.

The world runs fast.

But our souls run slow.

Our souls were designed for eternity, not the maddening pace of modern life. Dallas Willard observed that to pursue spiritual health, "You must ruthlessly eliminate hurry from your life." A nice thought. But our first response is, "Yeah, right. That's impossible."

The world has made it impossible to *not* hurry in some capacity. We are like skipping rocks—moving quickly enough that we stay on the surface. But the reality is that your soul does not move at that maddening pace. To go deep, to do the work of the soul, you must *slow down*.

Restoration and healing both happen slowly. It may sound impossible to eliminate hurry, but you can introduce slowness into particular areas of your life.

Committing to a year is actually not all that long considering what community and friendship were meant to be. Doing so opens up an opportunity for the slow work to take root . . . and grow beyond your wildest expectations. In fact, when the year is done, most aren't ready for it to be over. We've got you covered there as well. But more on that in due time.

While a year will go by fast, it doesn't come without challenges. Being part of a community involves the messiness of relationships. It will be difficult and feel downright impossible some days. A friend once joked that one of Jesus' most astounding miracles was that he had twelve close friends in his thirties. Honestly, maintaining two close friends is hard, let alone twelve. Like all good things in this world, community is opposed. Life isolates us. People are messy. And the kingdom of darkness isolates us. Satan's favorite technique to destroy the children of God is to divide and conquer. John 10:10 reads, "The thief comes only to steal and kill and destroy."

You will have to fight for this community as you build it with patience and intentionality. It's essential you push through because despite all the relational hurt, betrayal, disappointment, and loneliness, our souls cry out for a deep intimacy in fellowship. We have looked for it in many places: the clubs we belong to, the church groups, fraternities, even our own families.

One of the reasons that we continue to be drawn to church or small groups is because they are *almost* there. They offer a space where people with shared desire and beliefs gather. Yet we've seen these fellowships fail. Many men have been casualties of those shipwrecks.

But we haven't stopped there. We've attended conferences, joined book groups, taken Bible studies, and tried men's gatherings of every shape and size for one main reason—because we were made to be known and live in fellowship. Some of us have been burned by these groups so deeply that even uttering the name "small group" sends a shiver down our spines and tightens our chests. It reminds us of the pressure, the performance, the betrayal, and the *religiosity* that so often descends like gas in the trenches, choking out all possibility of genuine vulnerability and camaraderie.

Despite all the disappointment, community can be done well. While the opposition is real, so is the opportunity for what we long for. Authentic community that facilitates real fellowship, true healing, and deep communion with God is available. That's what we're after.

Movies that demonstrate this rare kind of community of men such as *The Fellowship of the Ring, Saving Private Ryan,* and *Ocean's Eleven* captivate us. And there's a reason for that. An often overlooked but essential fact about male friendship is that to have real community, you must have a shared mission. The fellowship of the ring would not exist without the mission to destroy the one ring and defeat the armies of Mordor. *Saving Private Ryan* has its shared mission right there in the title. In stories of old, the knights of the round table gathered around a single and mighty purpose. Male relationships do not work if the only shared mission *is* the relationship. Part of the Imago Dei men uniquely carry is God's *intervention.* Men are made to *act.* If all you ever do is sit in a circle and talk about your relationship, that fellowship will be disintegrated by the slightest adversity.

We need a shared mission. One built around the restorative work of Jesus Christ that's focused on advocating and fighting for each other's freedom, wholeheartedness, and deeper life with God.

That is our mission—and this plan offers the roadmap to spending a year of weeks with like-minded men. But as we've noted, fellowship requires adventure. So what do you actually *do?*

In the pages that follow, we lay out exactly what to do, how to do it, and when to do it. And you'll have a leader to keep things on track.

Speaking of leaders, throughout this guide, we've set aside pages where we talk directly to the leaders. These sections are called *Leader's Cairn* and address everything the leader needs to know to start and guide your group. Unless you're the leader, you're welcome to skip over these pages.

But first, it's essential that every man have a vision for the larger picture. So let's turn to some logistics. Men, it's time for your pre-mission briefing.

FIRST THINGS

You've been invited into this group by your leader. The men you'll be spending the next year with have also been hand-picked. While we've designed this guide with eight men in mind, you may have fewer or more in your group. Rest assured it's the right size for the journey God has planned for you over the next twelve months.

Your group's first objective is to establish a covenant of confidentiality. What's said in the group stays in the group. For honest conversation to happen, this is a non-negotiable.

It's also important that everyone in the group commit to the full year of meetings. Your first gathering should include a time of consecration to pray over your group and the coming year together. Bring it under the authority of Jesus and into his kingdom. This isn't just a formality. Remember, pursuing community and restoration is opposed. You must contend for it.

This consecration time is a chance to give all that is going to happen over the next year to God. It shouldn't sound like a government bill or be full of religious language. Keep it short, simple, and real. Here's an example you could use: *God, thank you for the gift of these men who are committed to taking this journey. We give ourselves to you. We surrender our agenda. We consecrate our year together and bring it under your authority, rule, and protection. We invite you in. Lead us. Guide us. We pray this in the name and authority of Jesus.*

Okay, with that, it's time to move into the first unit—the *Wild at Heart* video series. Whether it's your first time through or another pass, God has some big breakthroughs for you in the weeks to come.

We can promise you this: the coming year has the potential to be your best yet!

LEADER'S CAIRN

Every group will have a leader. Even if a group considers itself a collective of peers, someone initially made it happen—and will have to continue making it happen.

In your group, that is you!

Throughout this book, we'll offer what we refer to as cairns—stacked stones to help remind you what's essential as you navigate the unique terrain of this journey.

The cairns will offer additional information that individual members don't necessarily need to know but that will prove helpful for you, as leader, in navigating and guiding men through this year-long curriculum.

TWO KINDS OF GROUPS

As the leader, your first question might be, "How do I even get a group started?" You may have picked up this book without already having a group together but with the desire to spend a year with men in the fellowship of a shared purpose.

So how do you get one going?

First, you need to know your motive for starting a group. There are usually two kinds of groups and each requires something specific from you.

The first is a group of men who are roughly at the same place in their walk with God and in their journey of restoration. Perhaps they have gone through similar material or been to a Wild at Heart event. This group of men is already on a path and is simply looking for new material to work through. In this case, your role as a leader is minimal, and you should expect to be poured into and nourished along with the other men.

The second is a group of men who might not know each other very well and are new to the Wild at Heart message. Where each man is in their walk with God and season of life will vary. This may be their first time diving into the deep matters of the heart. In this case, your role as a leader will be significant as you guide some into their first encounters with their stories and the Story God is telling. Rather than being poured into, this situation requires you to pour into others, to serve, and to lead them into healing and deeper intimacy with God.

Once you've determined your motive for starting a group, use that as a touchstone for the kind of men you invite. Is there a man you are feeling called to go after? Are there a few guys you enjoy being around who, though they might not have the same experiences as you, are headed in a similar direction and want the same kind of spiritual life?

Your greatest tool in discerning which men to invite is your conversational intimacy with God. Pray about which men to invite. If hearing the voice of God is a new concept to you, it would be a good idea to pause before creating a group and go through the *Walking with God* book and video series or listen to the "Conversing with God" Wild at Heart podcast series (found on our website or through your favorite podcast app).

GROUP SIZE AND SPACE

How many men to include in your group will largely be dictated by your circumstances. You may only have a few men in your world that are pursuing the same kind of life that you are. That's okay. On the other hand, you may know dozens of men but if you invite too many, you no longer have a men's group, you have a church. In general, every group needs more than two men (so you're not alone if one can't make it) and no more than twelve (so everyone has time to talk).

The next step in creating a group is deciding on the space.

On a practical note, you will need access to a television as well as the internet. Each unit except one is built around a video or film series. You will watch the episode and then have a facilitated discussion around that content.

Other than the necessary technological equipment, choose a space that minimizes distraction. The point of each meeting is to facilitate discussion around core issues of each man's life and heart. We recommend that you choose a space that you can commit to for a year (not rotate week by week). A large garage or basement hang-out area works great. You just need a place that's casual, comfortable, free of interruptions, and allows for vulnerability.

BEFORE YOUR GROUP MEETS

There are a few logistical issues you'll want to be aware of before the first meeting.

First, it's smart to set up a group email list to communicate with the men as needed. This doesn't mean you need to send weekly emails, but there is a value in sending reminders, schedule changes, and planning emails throughout the year. So make sure this foundation is in place from before the first gathering.

As the leader, you will need to purchase in advance the *Wild at Heart*, *Becoming a King*, and HBO *Band of Brothers* series. The *Fathered by God* video series and opening video for *We All Have a Story* can be accessed free of charge. Find out more at WildatHeart.org/AYearwithMen.

We recommend you watch the video sessions ahead of time so you are familiar with the content, ready with any upfront comments, and know which discussion questions are best for your group.

Decide in advance whether you and your group will be reading through the relevant chapters of *Wild at Heart*, *Becoming a King*, and *Fathered by God* books—and if so, inform the men ahead of time so they can make sure they have the book before each unit begins.

If you have a smaller group of three or four, you will need to add an additional study at the end of Unit #2 (*We All Have a Story*) since it is planned for eight weeks based on eight men telling their stories. At the back of this book, we've provided additional group study options. Keep in mind that discussion questions for these optional studies are not included in this book . . . so it's good to determine that now and plan accordingly. If your group has more than eight men, you'll also need to extend Unit #2 accordingly, using the additional unscheduled weeks as needed.

Finally, an essential part of this year together is planning an adventure trip with your men. We recommend utilizing the summer months for this time away, but when it happens for your group depends on what time of the year you began this study.

As leader, you'll want to read the Adventure Together chapter early rather than winging it a few weeks before the trip. The chapter features insights into how to make the most of this trip. The main thing is to start early. It's best to nail things down several months in advance for group input (on price and type of activity), time to assign responsibilities for various parts of the trip, reserve the dates on everyone's calendar, and make reservations (if needed).

TIME CONSIDERATIONS

We recommend each gathering be around two hours but no less than ninety minutes. How you structure your time together will depend on the commitment that your group is willing to make.

Establish a start and stop time boundary to respect each man's time commitment as well as your own. Too many groups have lost members because the meetings start late and run long. If you agree to start at 7:00 and end at 9:00, then be intentional about it. The best way to prevent stragglers is to always start on time. You'll also want to note (to yourself at least) when it's about 15 minutes before the meeting wrap-up time and guide it to a smooth landing.

Praying at the beginning of your time will help center each man for the upcoming study and conversation. Make sure the focus of the time together is the study that the men prepared for. Be careful of small talk taking too much group time. As your fellowship deepens, greeting one another and getting updated on how everyone is doing could end up taking the whole time. So if you want to touch base with everyone before getting started, structure that upfront time as optional before the main meeting time or have the more casual conversation, for those who want it, at the end of each meeting.

Another excellent tool at your disposal to help center your group before each meeting is the free Pause App (you can find it in the App store). Go through the one-minute or three-minute pause together at the start of your session to center yourselves in Christ and release to Jesus what you are carrying into your time together.

You'll want to include time to pray and advocate for one another. Putting in the work and time to cultivate fellowship builds the rare and tremendous asset of having brothers-in-arms who lock shields and fight for one another. It's best to do this at the end of your session since you'll know more about where each man is after the conversation.

And remember, it's not all up to you. You'll lead best by following Jesus. So invite him in, walk with him, and look for his presence. Jesus loves to show up.

FIRST TIME TOGETHER

In your first meeting as a group, plan to spend the opening minutes consecrating your year together in prayer and laying down clear expectations.

As a community, what are you expecting from one another?

Is each man willing to not just show up for a year, but to arrive prepared by reading through any assigned content ahead of time? The group can only go as far and as deep as their shared commitment. So without being legalistic, go over the yearly plan together and make sure each man is clear on what's expected.

Affirm confidentiality. As stated earlier, the assurance should be what's said in the group stays in the group. You'll want to make clear, as leader, that this confidentiality doesn't extend to anyone sharing about a current situation where a spouse or child is in imminent harm or danger.

It would be a good idea to let each man briefly share his hopes and expectations for the year. What are they anticipating? What are they expecting? What are they hesitant about (perhaps based on previous men's groups)? Knowing what each man is bringing into the group offers valuable insight into how they will relate to you and the other men.

You'll want to limit the above so you have enough time for Session 1 of the *Wild at Heart* video series and the conversation that follows. Make sure your first time together sets a good precedent for starting and wrapping up at the promised time.

Remember, information for accessing or purchasing the video or film series associated with the five units of this study can be found at WildatHeart.org/AYearwithMen. You'll want to plan early for this essential aspect of the weekly meetings.

That's it for now. We'll continue the discussion in additional *Leader's Cairn* sections throughout the book.

UNIT #1

WILD AT HEART

Weeks 1–7

INTRODUCTION TO
Wild at Heart
BY JOHN ELDREDGE

The way a man's life unfolds most days is brutal on the heart. Endless hours at a computer screen, selling shoes at the mall, meetings, relentless texts, phone calls. The business world—where the majority of American men live and die—requires a man to be efficient and punctual. Corporate policies and procedures are designed with one aim: to harness a man to the plow and make him produce.

But the soul refuses to be harnessed; it longs for passion, for freedom, for *life*.

What messages have you been taught about what a man ought to be? Responsible? Sensitive? Disciplined? Dutiful? While these can be good qualities, they completely fail to offer any source of true strength or road map to deeper restoration.

They fail to stir our masculine heart because we need something more.

We need *permission*.

Permission to be what we are—men made in God's image. Permission to live from the heart and not from the list of what we should or ought to do has left men exhausted, burnt out, or simply *bored*.

Men know it, too, but are often unable to explain why their heart is missing. They know their heart is on the run, but they often do not know where to pick up the trail. The answer is simply this: We have not invited a man to know and live from his deep heart.

But God made the masculine heart, set it within every man, and thereby offers him an *invitation*: Come, and live out what I meant you to be. God *meant* something when he meant man, and if we are to ever find ourselves we must find that.

What has he set in the masculine heart? Instead of asking what you think you ought to do to become a better man, I want to ask, *What makes you come alive?* What stirs your heart?

In this first unit, we will lay the foundation of all that is to come by exploring the three core desires of a man's heart: a battle to fight, an adventure to live, and a beauty to love. Along the way, we will find God and an invitation into deeper restoration.

LEADER'S CAIRN

For the first six weeks of your time together, you will watch an episode of the *Wild at Heart* video series and use the following study guide questions to facilitate discussion. There are more questions provided than most groups will be able to get through. If each man is willing to speak his mind and share his heart, it doesn't take many questions to lead into rich terrain. It's always better to go deeper with fewer questions.

That being said, if you have gone through *Wild at Heart* before, you may want to choose a smaller number of questions that you want the group to start with. They may be questions that are speaking to you directly, or they may be the questions you think your men most need to work through.

The seventh week will be a week for your group to discuss the breakthroughs they've had individually as well as to process any of the content from this first unit.

Wild at Heart: Session 1
The Heart of a Man

WATCH

As a group, watch Session 1

READ (Optional)

Chapters 1 and 2 of *Wild at Heart*

SHARE

Choose from the following questions to help guide your conversation.

1. The movies you love are clues to the deep desires of your heart. What is your favorite movie? Why are you drawn to it?

2. Think back to your childhood—what kind of games did you like to play? What did you like about them?

3. The core desires of a man's soul are a battle to fight, an adventure to live, and a beauty to love. How do you see these three desires expressing themselves in your life?

4. Who is the man you feel you *ought* to be? When you think of a "good man" or a "Christian man," what is he like? Do you want to be like this person? Why or why not?

5. The image we have as God the Father is profoundly shaped by the man our earthly father was. How would you describe your dad . . . and how has that affected your view of God?

6. We can know the heart of the artist by what he creates. What does creation say about God? How do the North Sea, the outback of Australia, or the high country of the Rockies reflect aspects of God's personality?

Wild at Heart: Session 2
The Poser

WATCH

As a group, watch Session 2

READ (Optional)

Chapter 3 of *Wild at Heart*

SHARE

Choose from the following questions to help guide your conversation.

1. What in Bart's story stood out to you? Why?

2. Early in life, we learn what the world wants from us—and what it doesn't like. Where did you receive recognition early on as a boy? How did that shape what you pursued...and left behind?

3. As a man, what do you tend to avoid because it makes you feel weak, incompetent, or vulnerable? When did you first decide you weren't going to risk in this area—and why?

4. How would the people in your life describe you as a man? How would you describe yourself?

5. In the garden, when Adam realizes he has failed, he hides. Each son of Adam has followed suit. We hide behind our jobs, our hobbies, and our carefully constructed personalities. What is your fig leaf?

6. How has the question of whether you have what it takes as a man been answered in your life?

Wild at Heart: Session 3
The Wound

WATCH
As a group, watch Session 3

READ (Optional)
Chapters 4 and 7 of *Wild at Heart*

SHARE
Choose from the following questions to help guide your conversation.

1. What part of Pablo's story affected you? What did it bring up in you?

2. Did you know your dad adored you? What did you do together with your dad when you were a boy?

3. What was your dad's message to you in response to your question, "Do I have what it takes?" Did he answer a thousand times, "Yes!"?

4. What did your dad teach you about yourself as a man?

5. Every boy, in his journey to become a man, takes an arrow in the center of his heart, in the place of his strength. Because wounds are rarely discussed and even more rarely healed, every man has them. Name one of your childhood wounds.

6. What message was delivered with this wound? What did it communicate to you about yourself? What did you vow to yourself after it was delivered?

For a guided prayer through inner healing, visit WildAtHeart.org/prayer/prayer-inner-healing.

Wild at Heart: Session 4
The Battle

WATCH

As a group, watch Session 4

READ (Optional)

Chapters 8 and 9 of *Wild at Heart*

SHARE

Choose from the following questions to help guide your conversation.

1. What did Sam's story stir in your heart? Share why.

2. God set within every man a warrior heart. Did you see it in you as a boy?

3. Can you see your warrior heart now as a man? What gets you angry? What do you want to set right?

4. Have you considered spiritual warfare a category for the battles that have come against you? Why or why not?

5. What battle are you facing in your life right now? What are the stakes?

6. What is an agreement you've made that's holding you back? Are you willing to name it and break it right now?

Wild at Heart: Session 5
The Beauty

WATCH

As a group, watch Session 5

READ (Optional)

Chapter 10 of *Wild at Heart*

SHARE

Choose from the following questions to help guide your conversation.

1. Share what stood out to you about Alex's story.

2. What is your relationship like with the key women in your life (wife, daughter, mother)? How would you like to see that change?

3. Right now, at this point in your journey, are you hopeful about love and sexuality, or are you cynical? Why?

4. If you are married, how do you usually feel in the presence of your wife? Is it thrilled, loving, strong . . . or do you feel threatened? Like a boy?

5. How much of your life have you spent looking to the woman for validation? How has that gone for you?

6. What will it cost you to fight for the beauty in your life? Are you willing to do so?

A great way to understand the woman in your life is to read *Captivating*. Pick up a copy for her as well.

Wild at Heart: Session 6
The Adventure

WATCH

As a group, watch Session 6

READ (Optional)

Chapter 11 of *Wild at Heart*

SHARE

Choose from the following questions to help guide your conversation.

1. What most stands out to you about Morgan's story? Why?

2. What casual adventures are you pursuing?

3. What is your current crucial adventure? Why is this important to you?

4. How would you describe your critical adventure—where is God calling you to join him in changing the world?

5. What makes you feel most alive? How often do you make time to enter into this adventure?

6. Have you ever been faced with a choice between the reasonable path of practicality and the path toward a dream? Which did you choose? What happened?

Wild at Heart: Session 7
Writing the Next Chapter

There is no video for this session. It's a time for your group to look back over the past six weeks . . . and look ahead to life as the new man they are becoming.

SHARE

Choose from the following questions to help guide your conversation.

1. What is your biggest takeaway from this study? Why?

2. What is the biggest question you still have regarding this content?

3. What do you sense God wants to work with you on now? How will doing so make a difference in your life?

GET OUT AND DO

WEEK 8

Asking your body to exert itself in strenuous exercise beyond its capacity will cause it to break down. Your soul is no different. If *every single week* asks you to show up, to offer, to do the real work of pursuing restoration as well as masculine fellowship, you will get burnt out.

The soul has its rhythms. You cannot expect it to constantly perform without times of play and restoration.

Between each unit of your year together, you will spend your regular meeting time getting out and *doing* something. This offers a sense of transition and rest between each particular message, but it also serves a very real and necessary function of living life together. Remember, male relationships are built around a shared mission, and they are fed by *doing*—acting together. This doesn't need to be complicated. Here are a few ideas:

- Axe Throwing

This is so satisfying. Throwing something sharp and hearing it *thunk* into solid wood is therapy to the soul. It just feels good. Perhaps that's why axe throwing venues have popped up just about everywhere in recent years. Find one in your area and go throw some axes! It doesn't matter if you're good at it; all that matters is to have something real in your hand and hurl it. If you don't live near such an establishment but have the ability to set it up for yourself in a safe environment, go for it.

- Hiking

This isn't an option everywhere nor is it doable year-round, but if you have access to wilderness, get into it. Numerous studies have been done on the health benefits of nature and the results are what you'd expect. It is *really* good for you. The benefits to your body are wide ranging while the impact on your soul is immeasurable. Get together and get outside.

- Cigars or Brewery

We realize alcohol and tobacco aren't for everyone. Depending on the make-up of your group, this may or may not be a good option. But if it is, consider checking out a new brewery or introducing the guys to one of your favorites. Or grab some cigars from your local tobacconist and hang out at a backyard fire pit or a garage. "Command those who are rich in this present world not to be arrogant nor to put their hope in wealth, which is so uncertain, but to put their hope in God, who richly provides us with everything for our enjoyment" (1 Tim. 6:17).

- Rock Climbing

If you're not a rock climber, you can still have a good experience at your local rock climbing gym. They offer equipment rentals and will show you how to get started safely. Facing your fear of heights together can be an excellent way to build camaraderie. There are climbing routes designed for all skill levels. You do not need to be particularly fit or coordinated to climb a 5.5.

- Poker

All you need is a deck of cards and some poker chips. For guys that have never learned how to play, it's an excellent way to initiate them to the game. Rather than making it ultra-competitive or high stakes, make it a time for joy.

- Driving range

Even if some guys in your group have never golfed before, there is something immensely enjoyable about going to a driving range and hitting a few dozen golf balls into oblivion (or about 10 feet on the first couple tries).

These are just a few suggestions. Toss out what doesn't sound good. Try the others. Or come up with your own ideas of what to do that are a better fit for your men.

There is no *failing* at this. There are not better or worse options.

Because it may not sound *manly* doesn't mean it's not perfect for your particular group. Likewise, just because it seems manly doesn't mean it is the best way to experience camaraderie. It's not about competition among the men but bringing everyone together in a shared adventure.

The only requirement is that you are together and doing something other than talking. There needs to be some action involved, but that can span everything from board games to skydiving.

Now, go out and do something!

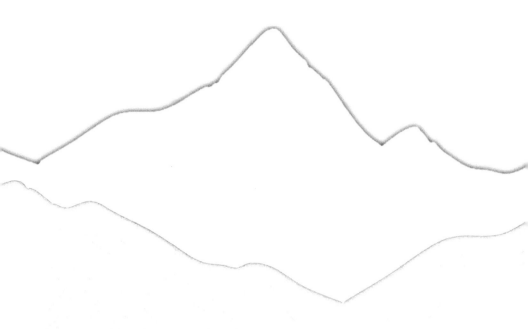

UNIT #2

WE ALL HAVE A STORY

Weeks 9–16

*Groups with fewer than eight men will need to add another unit during the remaining weeks. Groups with nine or more men will need to add a week per additional man.

INTRODUCTION TO
We All Have a Story

You'll want to read this chapter in full before the first meeting of this unit.

The basis of any good relationship—friendship, a band of brothers—is knowing one another's story.

But if that's true, why do so few people know the stories of those closest to them? Quite simply, people never ask!

Yet everyone has a story. And it is filled with victories, heartbreaks, love, loss, and mystery. All of these components have shaped us into the men we are today. You can't have deep conversations about God or yourself if you don't understand your story. Nor can you truly know the men in your group until you understand their stories.

To advocate and fight for one another, you must know each other's story.

But this skill doesn't just happen. We must discover how to know and then tell our stories and how to listen well to other men's stories.

For this unit, each man will share his life story with the other men in your group—and have the sacred honor of hearing and responding to each other's stories. Your leader will go first, to model what it looks like for a man to tell his story.

Because the sharing of stories is a courageous and deeply vulnerable act, it's essential we learn the ways to tell our story well . . . and how to listen well to the stories of others.

In the rest of the chapter, we'll cover the following:

- Part 1: Knowing Your Story
- Part 2: Telling Your Story
- Part 3: Listening to a Man's Story
- Part 4: Responding to a Man's Story

LEADER'S CAIRN

During this unit of your year together, each man will tell his story. It matters deeply. Knowing and telling his story is one of the most important things a man can do.

To prepare, have each man read the following four-part section on how to know his story, tell his story, listen to the stories from other men, and respond to those stories in a helpful way. Both are a craft that takes time to learn; both can be handled well … or poorly. To make this a positive experience, it is essential that each man take it seriously.

This unit will last as many weeks as you have men in your group. If you have eight men (including you), then it will be an eight-week unit. **The first week's session will begin with John's short opening video (the only video for this unit), followed by you telling your story.** If you have more than eight men, this unit will require an additional week for each additional man. If you have four or fewer men, you will need to add another unit after every man has told his story. You'll find other study options in the last section of this book.

It's essential that every man have one full session to tell his story. You'll need to decide as a group how long you want to give each person to tell his story. This will be based on how long each week's gatherings are, but ideally each man would have 45 minutes to an hour to tell his story and at least a half hour for discussion. We go into why this matters later, but you need to make an upfront agreement as a group and then stay consistent from man to man.

We recommend you, as leader, go first with your story. You will not be able to model how to offer feedback, but it is more important to lead in vulnerability. Dan Allender says, "You can only take someone else as far as you have gone yourself." You cannot take someone to a place that you have not been to first.

As the leader, set the tone for others. As the leader, model maturity. Offer to your men what they can handle and let them see you. Name what is worth naming. Even just a little bit of reflection on how to tell your story by modeling it can set the group up for success.

From there, it's best to pray and ask God (as a group) what order the men should go in to tell their story. Often the man most eager to go isn't necessarily the best person to start. Other men will try and go last. The only way to know the optimal order is to ask God and model listening prayer for the group.

We've found it beneficial for each man to bring in a photo of himself as a boy when it is their turn to tell their story. Having that picture gives others a doorway to enter into the story. This can be a powerful exercise.

There is a four-part Wild at Heart podcast series that discusses how to tell your story and how to listen to another's story. This resource will be immensely helpful to you as the leader and as an optional resource for men between gatherings. You can find all four episodes at WildatHeart.org/AYearwithMen.

PART 1: KNOWING YOUR STORY

Story isn't just something we're drawn to. Your life is a story. And the best way for your group of men to understand who you are is to take them through key events of your life . . . *as* a story.

Of course, the first step to sharing your story begins with *knowing* your story.

Let's start with this simple prayer. It will help lift the fog of the world and bring light to your story.

Jesus, I consecrate my life and my story to you. I ask for clarity in my story. You commanded, "Let there be light." Let there be light

*in my story; banish the fog and all obscuring. I ask for a spirit of
wisdom and revelation. I ask to be hidden in your love. I take refuge
in your love. I bring the authority of Jesus Christ and the full work
and glory of Christ against all spiritual opposition, I cut it off in the
name of the Lord, and I forbid it to operate here. Lead me, Jesus,
into what you have for me today. Amen.*

For this exercise, you'll want to set aside at least an hour of uninter-
rupted time and have a journal or device to remember and write down
key moments of your past. Aim for five to ten significant events or memories from your childhood (roughly ages 0–13), five to ten from young
adulthood (14–27), and five to ten from adulthood (28–present),
breaking down adulthood memories by decade.

You don't need to do all of this at once; take your time and be aware
of how much your heart can handle. Spread it out over the course of a
week if you need to. It may also be helpful to have a photo of yourself
at each of these stages available. Ponder that person. How do you feel
about him?

Do not be intimidated by this practice if you are not into journaling
or if you've never done an exercise like this before. You do not need to
write complete sentences or beautiful prose. Just get down enough to
know which memory you mean. It can simply be a few words: "move
from Springfield," "picture day," "the pull-up bar."

Now look back through your list of events and memories, taking one
season of life at a time. Which ones evoke a strong emotional response?

As you think about your childhood, what were the high points, the
low points, and the major shifts that occurred? It might be helpful to
rate them using the following scale: -10 through +10 with -10 = Most
Negative and +10 = Most Positive.

Think about your home life, about your mom and dad, about your
family. What was it like to grow up in your family? How was your home
life? What were you rewarded for? Being smart? Being athletic? Being out
of the way and not a problem? What were you shamed for? What were your
dreams? What were your battles and adventures? Who did you long to be?

Now turn to your young adulthood and ask the same thing: What were the memories of blessing and what were the memories of harm? What were some major shifts that occurred?

Thinking about what love was like for you, how was your heart broken? How were your questions or beliefs about sex rewarded or shamed?

Next, consider adulthood: What were some high points, low points, and major shifts that occurred? While this season is the longest, it is the earlier seasons that often shape us the most. Name how earlier seasons shaped your significant memories as an adult. How have the messages and recurring themes from childhood and young adulthood been reaffirmed? Have they played out in new ways in adulthood? What significant failures and successes have you experienced?

Finally, turn to your current moment. Consider how this moment is a result of the sum of the significant moments from your past. How is your life the result of the story? How do your childhood dreams correspond to your current disappointments?

What are you longing for? What do you want to see in your life? What are your current battles? What are the adventures you want to be in? What does love look like in your life? What is the healing you want? How is your story now unfolding?

Returning to the whole picture: If you don't have many memories from a period of your life such as childhood, ask yourself why? If you don't want to go to a specific time or would rather avoid specific memories, seek to understand why. The same if you find yourself trying to blow past a period of your life or minimize it or feel angry with certain memories. The gold is there, but you have to mine it.

PART 2: TELLING YOUR STORY

Preparing to tell your story in a group context will actually help reveal your story to you. And the questions and responses from those in your group will shine even more light on it.

This is how God designed it to be.

We are made for community rather than to do life on our own. When it comes to your story, those close to you—especially those who walk with God—can often provide insights into how you've been shaped by the people and events in your life. Certainly the most qualified individual to help in these matters is a trained professional, therapist, counselor, or pastor. But if your group members take this guide seriously, it can be a tremendously rewarding experience.

But like most good things in life, this isn't easy.

It can be difficult to share stories of betrayal, bad choices, loss, and abuse. You might not have a completely firm grasp on it yourself and that's okay. Perhaps it's difficult for you to speak in a group context. Sharing requires risk and vulnerability.

Proper preparation and the right expectations can go a long way in making the experience go well. Here are some helpful insights as you think through how best to share your story.

- **You Need Structure**

Keep in mind that there will be a time limit to telling your story. Your leader will confirm how long you'll have—likely 45 minutes to an hour. Sticking to a set time limit allows you to focus on what you know is crucial to your story. As you practice and prepare, make sure the stories you want to tell fit within that time frame.

Structure your talk so that you don't burn all your time in one season. You'll be surprised at how fast 45 minutes or an hour goes. It would be disappointing to be somewhere in fourth grade and be told that you are out of time. Your group will all assume something happened in the next 30 years, but they won't know what. Plus, you will not feel seen or known if you spend all of your time on only one part of your life.

We offer an exercise at the end of this chapter that is a helpful place to start in preparing to tell your story. It will make establishing a structure much easier. For now, a good way to give yourself structure is to divide up your life between seasons.

If you have 45 minutes, give 15 minutes of time to share about your childhood years, spend the next 15 minutes on adolescence and young adulthood, and give your last 15 minutes to adulthood. You might have more to share from one season of life than another, so it is perfectly okay to be flexible. But be intentional about getting to each life season.

Once you determine the best way to share your story, write it down and bring it with you. When you get to the actual moment of sharing your story, it will be helpful to have prepared notes or simple cues to remind you where you are and where you want to go. Keep these notes simple so that it is easy to stay on track.

- Practice

Practicing beforehand may feel strange, but it can go a long way in helping you feel ready to share your story with others. You might be surprised at how quickly you run out of time or how much time you have left to fill.

You don't need to write out a script or read your story word for word to your group. But it is helpful to get a feel for how long the stories might take by going over what you plan to say. Making time to sit with your story beforehand will actually help you feel less vulnerable—especially when sharing hard stories from your past. Which brings us to the next point.

- Vulnerability

To be seen and to be known requires you to take some risks.

The longing to be known is primal. It is core to the human experience. To get there, you are going to have to risk. You will not be known if you only go an inch deep.

But you may be surprised by where the line of vulnerability actually is. Most people think that they have to share *a lot* of details to be truly vulnerable. The image most of us have of vulnerability is being on an operating table where our inmost being is exposed.

Vulnerability doesn't have to look like that. It might be that you need to dial down what you share to feel comfortable and safe. It may be as simple as a particular reaction to a story or naming a particular disappointment—and you can do that without naming too many details.

An immensely helpful place to start when deciding just how vulnerable you want to be is to ask God, "What should I share?"

● **What to Tell**

Frankly, it can be difficult to decide what to include in your time. One hour—or even half a day—isn't enough to cover every part of your life story.

You simply do not have time to tell it all. So take the pressure off to do so.

But there are some essential elements that you should address in order for others to know you. How much you share about them is up to you, but be intentional about addressing them. Having already gone through the *Wild at Heart* film sessions, some of these will be easier to name.

● **Why You Are the Way You Are**

Think about the current moment and work backwards. As you are telling your story, bring people up to speed on the person they are meeting now as the sum of the stories, the hopes, expectations, and high and low moments of your life. That will help them understand the tears or facial expressions or moments of silence when you get to certain parts of your story.

● **Your Wounding**

Wounding is essential in sharing your story because of the weight it carries in our lives and because of how much it has shaped us. The person we cultivate is too often in response to wounds we have received.

● **The Messages You Live Under**

Explaining the messages you live under and how your story delivered those messages will unlock for others why you are the way you are and why they experience you the way that they do. What are you saying to yourself when you look in the mirror? What feels true *right now*?

- Your False Self

We present the world with what we think it wants and hide who we are because we have already been told that's not it. Explaining the ways that you have constructed a false self and live from that place as a poser will help others understand your story and who you are now.

- Your Dreams and Desires

It's not all about loss and heartbreak. If people are to know you, they also need to know the great desires of your heart—what you dream of doing, what brings you joy, where you feel most alive and passionate. Be sure to share this aspect of who you are as well.

- Love

Who were your first loves and first heartbreaks? What does love look like right now? Are you living alone? Do you have a family? How has love played out in your story? These experiences shape how we offer our hearts to others in relationships, no matter the level of intimacy.

- Your Family of Origin

If others are going to know you, they need to know what it was like for you growing up. They need to know something about your mom, your dad, your family setting. You don't have to discuss areas you don't feel safe going into, but you do need to give some context for what it was like growing up in your home.

- Your Current Moment

Your story is not just something that happened in the past. It is happening *right now*. How you want your life to look from this point forward speaks volumes about who you are, how God is working in your life, and what makes your heart come alive. How can others know you if they do not know what you are facing right now and what course you are charting for yourself?

- Consider Your Expectations and Motives

As it comes time for you to tell your story, consider what expectations and motives you are bringing into the time and what you are expecting people's responses to be. What's your motive in wanting to be heard? Is it to make everyone love you? Is it to make sure you don't sound stupid? Remember, the goal isn't to impress the group. It is to be real and to be known.

- Don't Try to Put a Bow on It

People's lives are messy. Your life is messy. There are parts of your life that do not make sense. There is hurt that has not received healing. There are deep disappointments and places of confusion. Sometimes we have to tell ourselves that everything is fine so we are not overwhelmed by our grief. But ignoring it is not healthy for our hearts.

- What If Your Heart Is Mishandled?

There's a chance as you're sharing that someone will respond with an insensitive question or offer advice to fix everything in a clumsy or wrong way. If this happens to you, we are so sorry. This is a broken world with messy people. This is the risk. You're not sitting down with a room of therapists but a group of ordinary men.

If something is mishandled, your first response should be to say something, either in the moment or before your next gathering. The safest and most comfortable approach might be to talk with the group leader privately, afterwards, or before meeting as a group again. If you happen to be the leader and this happens to you, talk with someone you trust outside of the group.

The second action is to take your heart to God. A good prayer is, *Jesus, catch my heart.* As you're driving away from your time or as you're walking home, *Jesus, catch my heart, catch my heart, catch my heart.*

If you feel you weren't understood, ask for God's interpretation of what happened and for what is true about you. *Jesus, how did that go? Interpret that for me.* Your interpretation may be that it was a disaster, but that might not be God's interpretation at all. We also have an enemy who wants to jump in and put his toxic spin on things. Ultimately, what matters most is God's interpretation. So ask him and rest in what he says.

We just covered a lot of ground on how to tell your story. Now we'll turn our attention to another essential aspect of this process: how to listen to someone else's story.

PART 3: LISTENING TO A MAN'S STORY

How to listen well is an art that requires wisdom and practice.

One of the primal desires of the human heart is to be known. Yet we have all been hurt in that pursuit. The questions "Will I be seen?" and "Will I be handled well?" are always being asked in some way, and too often the answer has been *no*.

Sharing stories in a group of committed men can bring healing as well.

Because our hearts have been mishandled before, and because the sharing of stories is a courageous and deeply vulnerable act, you must learn how to listen well and respond well when someone's story is being shared.

Here are suggestions for being a good listener.

- Create a Safe Environment

The first step to listening well to someone's story is incredibly simple yet often overlooked: creating a safe environment.

People will be far more vulnerable in the context of a living room or a warm garage than they will in a coffee shop or a restaurant. Make sure the setting for these times is a place free of interruptions and where others outside of the group won't overhear.

Next, affirm from the beginning that this space is wholly confidential. Every member of the group must explicitly agree that what is shared in the group will not be repeated to others outside of the group (including spouses). For the level of safety that is required to access and share vulnerable stories, establish confidentiality.

- Minimize Distraction

It's best to turn your cellphone off. At the very least, put it on airplane mode or any other mode that inhibits the phone from ringing or receiving calls or texts. Even if your phone is silent, you still can't be present to someone's story if your phone is buzzing in your pocket.

Tell your family or friends what you are doing so they know that they won't be able to reach you during the designated time.

Think through other possible distractions—background noise, music, people walking through the space, windows overlooking outside activity or a busy street—unique to your particular environment and eliminate them.

- Set a Time Limit

It may feel wrong at first, but creating a sacred environment requires establishing a time limit and sticking to it.

Give 45 to 90 minutes per person. In the counseling world, this practice is called containment. It feels insensitive to tell someone that they only have ten minutes left to share while they are in the middle of a story, but it is actually loving. It establishes a uniquely protected space.

To say "You have this amount of my time" is to say "You have my full and undivided attention." It is for a limited time, but during that time you have the dignity of each person's full attention and presence.

Honoring a time limit affects how others in the group interpret their own time of sharing. How group members are treated in comparison to one another will not go unnoticed and sends a clear message. If one person shares for 45 minutes and is given little response time, and the next person shares for three hours and receives engaged feedback, the first person is going to be deeply wounded.

Place a specific time limit on the response time as well for the same reasons.

Provide at least 30 minutes to an hour to respond to someone's story. Not protecting the response time can send an even stronger message of *unseen* and *unheard* than not containing the time for the story itself.

Keep in mind the time allocated for a person's story and the response time need to fit within the pre-established start and stop time for the weekly gatherings. The leader will need to be the one who keeps everyone aware of the time so things stay on track.

- **Be Aware of Spiritual Opposition**

The Enemy and the kingdom of darkness do not want any of this to happen. You must pray. You must fight for the space and for one another. You must partner with God in resisting all spiritual opposition.

Pray during the week before your time, during the day of your group meeting, before the person tells his story, and again when your time is done. You might even need to pause to advocate for the man as he is telling his story if he is clearly under assault.

Remember, a move toward love, healing, or redemption is always opposed. A good prayer before the individual begins his story would be something like this:

> *Jesus, we give ourselves to you: our spirits, souls, and bodies, our hearts, minds, and wills. We take our place on your cross, dying with you to our sin and flesh, in your resurrection, in your victory and life, and in your ascension, in your authority, dominion, and rule. We consecrate this space to you, Jesus; we consecrate this time to you. We bring this time under your authority and rule. We bring the authority and rule of the Lord Jesus Christ against every foul spirit or device of wickedness coming against this time* [name specifically what you are sensing in the spirit is the particular assignment against the speaker]. *We cut them off in the name of Jesus and forbid them to operate here. By the cross of Christ, we silence all accusation from us and we forbid the Enemy to interpret this time. We take refuge in the love of Christ and bring this time under the love of Christ. We ask your angels to build a canopy of protection over us. In Jesus' name.*

Entering into one another's story is an opportunity to advocate for one another. You will be amazed at how much better your time will go when you fight for one another through prayer, using the authority you have in Christ. Use it.

Besides praying over the time itself, be aware of how the particular spiritual warfare assigned against the individual man's life will try to interfere with your ability to intervene on his behalf. If he's always felt people are bored by him or irritated at him, you'll want to guard against similar feelings as he speaks.

- ## Do Not Interrupt the Speaker

What the man shares in his story might evoke a strong emotion in you. It's okay to feel it, but don't interrupt the story being told.

A story might bring up a similar experience from your story—do not interject with "that happened to me too!" or speak out your own experience. That might feel like you are trying to identify with the speaker, but in reality you are derailing the person's momentum and co-opting the attention for yourself and your own story. Of course you can react, "Whoa, that's heavy. Please go on. I'd like to hear more," but do not steal the attention or time.

Do not ask questions, even if they are meant to clarify.

Don't move to fix. Many hearts have been missed by others trying to fix their stories quickly with simple answers or by interjecting unhelpful platitudes. The speaker might be entering into some of the wounding and agreements of his life, and someone else might interject, "Well, that's not what your inheritance is" or "That's not what I think of you. That's not what anyone in this group thinks of you," or "That's not true; John 1:12 says that you're a child of God."

Despite all good intentions, the message of such interjections is that you are uncomfortable and that you want them to quickly button up their problems. Perhaps you feel uncomfortable in difficult spaces and are seeking to squelch all suffering so that you don't have to confront it. You must be comfortable with messy. The more you can be okay with messy, the better you will be at handling other people's hearts.

Refuse to be a distraction. Release your particular gifting. Release your agenda. Remember, this time is not about you.

Do not hand the person a tissue unless he asks for one. It may sound bizarre, but not handing the speaker a tissue is practiced in counseling programs. When the man telling his story is experiencing intense emotion and there are tears and snot, do not hand over or offer a tissue. Do not move to comfort. The message that it sends is for the person speaking to get that emotion buttoned up quick, that their emotion is not okay nor welcome, and that they need to pull themselves together.

- Active Listening

Don't interrupt the speaker but do make an effort to communicate that you are fully present and actively engaged.

When the speaker makes eye contact with you, return his gaze, nod. As he is telling his story, make verbal affirmations that communicate you are tracking with the emotional tenor of the story. It's okay to laugh at funny or delightful moments, moan and grimace at moments of pain and anguish, and sound the affirmative "Mmm" of active and engaged listening.

A subtle practice that can communicate volumes is your body posture. Let your body posture mirror the body posture of the person sharing his story. Doing so communicates to the speaker that you are tracking on the same emotional wavelength. It will put him more at ease. It shows that you are present.

A man might share a detail from his childhood that you want to return to during the response time, but something said in the first five minutes will be difficult to remember an hour later. Take mental notes or jot down key phrases or questions you can save for the right time.

- What to Listen For

While the men in your group are telling their stories, there are some key elements to pay attention to. People's stories are varied and complex, infinitely so. But there are some common elements that weave through all of our stories.

How they play out are unique to the individual. The gift of working through one another's story in the context of a relationship is that we are able to see events and themes in other people's lives much more clearly than they do. What we live with on a daily basis is so close to us that we often cannot get the distance to see it clearly.

• Patterns and Themes

This is the most straightforward piece to listen for and requires you to look at the bigger picture. Patterns and themes are what come up over and over again. It can be a phrase they always say, a certain way of viewing themselves or others, or a struggle they can't overcome. Noting that can be one of the most helpful elements to understanding the person and in offering helpful observation during the response time.

• The Man's Glory

The patterns of people's stories often reveal their glory. You can discover the gifting God has given a person by paying attention to what has been repeatedly assaulted in his life.

• Wounds

To truly know someone, you must understand how they have been wounded, and how those wounds have shaped the way that person interacts with the world.

The wounds and the messages also carry with them an agreement or vow. If the message is "You are not worth being seen," the vow might be "Then I will not be seen" or perhaps "I will hide." If the message is "You are on your own," then the vow may be "I will not need anyone for anything."

A person's story often reveals the vows they've made but may not be aware of.

• Agreements

Because agreements don't *feel* like agreements but simply the facts, they can be extremely difficult to uncover for ourselves. Often, it is the observation, made in love by someone else, that reveals them. And when they are uncovered, there can be a lot of pushback. Agreements can be hard to break because sometimes we find solace in them (as hard as that is to believe) or simply believe they are true because we've lived under them for so long.

- Repeated Phrases

Important pieces of a person's story are sometimes revealed by the phrases we repeatedly use without thinking. Phrases about how a man feels towards himself or a particular season, choices, or relationships.

- How It's Said

How a man chooses to tell his story communicates as much or more than what's actually said. Notice, for instance, if important details or periods of his life are brushed over. Be aware of an absence of emotion during the sharing of loss. A man's tone conveys volumes.

- The False Self

From the place of our woundedness, we construct a false self. We find a few gifts that work for us, and we try to live off them. As you listen to someone's story, pay attention to how the false self, or poser, has been constructed.

- Dreams and Desires

When the man is sharing about his childhood, what were his dreams? What did he want to grow up to be? We are more likely to admit closely held dreams of the heart when they are framed in childhood because it's in childhood when we feel the most permission to dream.

Pay attention to what makes a man come alive, for that is the blueprint of his heart.

- Love and Sex

No matter how the story has turned out, what role love has played in our lives shapes how we interact with others and how we view the world. As you listen to the person's story, what did he learn about love? How was his heart broken? Who were the significant people in this story?

Something as rich and as beautiful as sex has been assaulted and broken in all of our lives. What has sexuality looked like in his life?

- **The Current Moment**

As the speaker begins to reach the end of his story, consider how his story has led up to the present. Notice how his current life is a result of his story.

It can be both positive and negative. How have his wounds and agreements contributed to his disappointments and pains? How have his glory and desires led to success and celebration? Without a doubt, it is all connected.

PART 4: RESPONDING TO A MAN'S STORY

By sharing his story, the man has offered you an incredible gift. It is holy ground.

But it gets even better. Because we can do more than just hear another's story. We can respond.

The very first response when a man finishes his story should be to thank him for his vulnerability, express honor at hearing the story, and affirm the courage, trust and emotional labor it took to tell it. After thanking the man for his vulnerability, see how he is doing emotionally. Some people might be okay afterwards; others are a complete mess.

Once you have checked in with the person and addressed any immediate concerns, you should shift into responding to what you heard in the man's story. A great way to start this is the simple phrase, "I heard you and this is what it did for me [then briefly explain]. Thank you."

This is the time to gently tease out more information through naming what you noticed and asking questions. Tell him the patterns and themes you saw in his life. Affirm the glory of the man's life and the giftings you see. With love and patience, perhaps address a wound you saw. Make him aware of a deep agreement that he might be living under. Point out repeated phrases. Remind him of his childhood dreams and desires. If you saw where in the story the man lost heart, ask questions about that. Talk about love and sex in his story if the man is comfortable going to that place. Investigate where there seem to be holes in the story, or where memory should be but isn't. Return to moments that really stood out to you or times of intense emotion.

Love covers a multitude of sins. If your response is truly out of love, it will be good. Even if it's not amazing or the key to his breakthrough, it will be saturated with grace because your motives are good.

Also, don't hesitate to admit the awkwardness. You can say, "I'm not a counselor and I'm not even sure that all that I'm feeling right now is true. But when I was listening to your story, I heard . . . "

This isn't about perfection.

Remember, the man is the focus. The ultimate goal of someone sharing his story is to be seen and known. Not for you to be amazing. You do not need to earn your seat at the table. This is not a quiz of how insightful you are or how loving you are. There is nothing to be proven. It's more than enough for you to offer the simple words, "Wow, I'm so sorry," or "That was profound. Thank you for sharing," or "That is the saddest thing I've ever heard."

During the time of response, it might be very appropriate to pray. That might look like helping the person break agreements, bringing healing to a wound, praying against a spiritual assignment set against the man's life, or praying for more restoration and integration. There is more content on this topic in John Eldredge's book *Waking the Dead* and in the Four Streams audio series at wildatheart.org. But there's no formula. There doesn't always need to be a closing time of prayer ministry. Often the healing comes simply in being heard or through thoughtful responses.

After the response and questions and prayer have happened, be sure to finish well. Come back around to the person who shared and check in. Ask him how he is. He may be angry, feel missed, or be doing really well. Acknowledge those feelings and offer any final thoughts.

As you leave, release everyone and everything to God. Do not try to carry any man, how the time went, or anything from the person's story. A great way to do this is to pray: *I bring the cross of Christ and the blood of*

Christ between me and every person [name them], *between me and every man's story. I give everyone and everything to you, Jesus. I give everything and everyone to you. I release them to you.*

At the end of the day, every person simply wants to be heard. So as you hear someone's story, listen with intention. That's it. And give yourself grace. Responding well is an art that takes time and practice to learn.

GET OUT AND DO
WEEK 17

With the completion of our last unit, this is a week to do something active as a group. If you're looking for ideas, check out the list provided in Week 8.

There's no pressure for this to be amazing. It's just a chance to enjoy time together around an activity.

Make it fun!

UNIT #3

BECOMING A KING

Weeks 18 – 23

INTRODUCTION TO
Becoming a King
BY MORGAN SNYDER

> "This is what the LORD says: Stand at the crossroads and look; ask for the ancient paths, ask where the good way is, and walk in it, and you will find rest for your souls" (Jeremiah 6:16).

G. K. Chesterton suggested that every generation loses the gospel and every generation is charged with its recovery. The ancient paths are lost to each generation of men, and it is up to each new generation to rediscover these ancient paths. This rediscovery, God's mission to bring restoration to all things, does not start in a global theater. It begins with you. It begins personally and intimately in the heart of every man. And you are not alone in pursuing this rediscovery of God's mission.

At the center of the gospel, at the heart of God's rescue of his creation and relationship with us, is God's intention to entrust us with power and to invite us to participate in the ongoing creativity of creation. The question God is asking is, "Can I trust you with power?" And the question of every man is, "Can I be trusted with power?"

All too often we have seen that the answer to those two questions is "no."

While driving through southern California, I saw enormous palm trees—glorious fronds lacing the cerulean sky. But these trees had grown so tall that they could not support their own weight. Intricate scaffolding built out of 2x4s spiderwebbed the palms, propping them up, supporting their weight. Without them, they would come crashing down. Easy access to water had made their roots shallow and weak.

This is the life of so many men: propped up lives, propped up relationships, propped up kingdoms. Without deep roots, the kingdoms and lives we build for ourselves are fragile and require us to prop them up with whatever we find that works: sports, the validation of others, alcohol, an affair.

It is easy and tempting to believe that the problems of our lives are external—the broken car, the broken career, the broken marriage. But these external problems reveal internal fissures: Why is it so frustrating when the car *does* break down? Why are you set off by a few words?

The external reveals that if we dig a little deeper, we will discover that we are men in need of excavation and reconstruction.

Jesus promises a way forward and invites us to follow him into his kingdom and into deeper whole-heartedness. But you would not be the first person to feel unsure of the way into the life that Jesus is offering.

Becoming a King is the fruit of almost two decades of being committed to excavation, to becoming the kind of soil that grows deep roots. That included sitting at the feet of many sages who have walked this path before us and learning from them.

The video series and following discussion questions offer a map to the ancient path of becoming the kind of trustworthy king to whom God can entrust the care of his kingdom. The kind of man who can be entrusted with power.

We arrive now at this central question: How do we become a king who is wholeheartedly consented to the authority, power, and partnership of the heart of God?

God cares far more about who you are than what you do. Who you become is more important than what you achieve. Who you are choosing to become may very well be the most important choice you ever make.

LEADER'S CAIRN

For this part of your year together, you will take your men through the video series of *Becoming a King* by Morgan Snyder.

Morgan is a key member of the Wild at Heart team and has been a warrior on the front line of this message for decades. His book shares the hard-won wisdom he has accumulated over the years and the wisdom gained from pursuing mentors during that time.

As you did for *Wild at Heart*, each week your group will watch an episode and then use the following questions to facilitate conversation. Depending on your time, you might not get to every question, so pick four or five that appear the most pertinent for your guys.

Becoming a King: Session 1
Becoming Powerful

WATCH

As a group, watch Session 1

READ (Optional)

Chapter 1 of *Becoming a King*

SHARE

Choose from the following questions to help guide your conversation.

1. The story God is telling is one in which he entrusts us with power. What are some childhood memories where you felt powerful?

2. Think of one man in particular (someone you know personally or not) who is a compelling model of a good king. What qualities do you admire in him? Why?

3. In the video, Morgan explains that each man is entrusted with a kingdom. Describe what your kingdom looks like right now.

4. Bring to mind the people under your authority and under your care—a partner, children, employees, certain friends. What do you hope they will one day be able to say about the impact of your life on theirs?

5. What is the state of your kingdom right now? Describe the condition of your kingdom. How are the people doing who are under your care? What about the physical aspects of your kingdom?

6. Dallas Willard noted, "Actions reveal beliefs one hundred percent of the time." What do your actions reveal about your beliefs? What are your underlying motives and fears and how do they motivate you? What are the core beliefs associated with these motives?

Becoming a King: Session 2
Becoming a Son

WATCH

As a group, watch Session 2

READ (Optional)

Chapter 2 of *Becoming a King*

SHARE

Choose from the following questions to help guide your conversation.

1. How have you been taught "father"? Who were the father figures in your life growing up, the good and the bad? Your father and/or stepfather, your coaches, teachers, pastors, etc. Without filtering yourself, how would you describe the traits of these men?

2. George MacDonald said, "The hardest, gladdest thing in the world is to cry Father! from a full heart . . . . The refusal to look up to God as our Father is the one central wrong in the whole human affair; the inability, the one central misery." How could crying out to God as Father be the gladdest thing? Why does it feel like the hardest thing right now?

3. God refuses to let you remain fatherless. In what ways might God be raising this issue of fatherlessness in your heart? What is not working in your life? What are you currently doing with what is not working?

4. How would you respond if you *knew* that it wasn't up to you to make life work? If you knew that there was someone at every turn ready to offer strength, power, protection, provision, affection, and leadership? Would that change the way you are living right now?

5. Looking back at your story through the lens of God fathering you, what were ways that God was fathering you, even if you did not know it at the time, or were not able to receive it?

6. One close friend confessed to Morgan, "I feel behind just about everywhere. I feel behind in my marriage, behind in my finances. I even feel behind in my landscaping!" It was a courageous confession that many men share. Do you feel "behind" in any area of your life?

Becoming a King: Session 3
Becoming the Man You Were Born to Be

WATCH

As a group, watch Session 3

READ (Optional)

Chapter 4 of *Becoming a King*

SHARE

Choose from the following questions to help guide your conversation.

1. How do you hide? What is the false self that you have constructed to make life work?

2. If the people in your life who are closest to you were asked to describe you, what do you fear they would say?

3. Each of us carries the question, "Am I a real man?" Who are the people that you are taking this question to?

4. The questions "Am I the real deal? Am I worthy of love and belonging?" haunt us. Where are you bringing these questions to be answered?

5. What is it that makes your heart come alive? What are the stories, adventures, roles, and experiences that move you? When have you felt most like your truest self?

6. Describe your true self. Who is the man you are working to become? What is he like? What do you hope people will say of the man you will be and his impact in his world?

Becoming a King: Session 4
Becoming a Generalist

WATCH

As a group, watch Session 4

READ (Optional)

Chapter 5 of *Becoming a King*

SHARE

Choose from the following questions to help guide your conversation.

1. What is your reaction to the story of a Native American chief who responded after American colonists in the 1700s "generously" offered to educate several of his tribe's boys? How did the founders of our nation and Native Americans think differently about the ways to "educate" young men? Does this story relate to your own?

2. In what areas of your life do you feel strong when you are in the company of men? What are the circumstances and what are the men like that allow you to feel strong?

3. In what areas of your life do you feel uncomfortable or weak in the company of men? What are the circumstances and what are the men like that make you feel uncomfortable or weak?

4. Think of a time when you saw a man demonstrating a fierce mastery (a mechanic working on a car, a teacher presenting a compelling idea, a heroic figure in a film). What did you admire about this man and why? What does it bring up in you?

5. What aspects of you as a man feel the most atrophied and in need of restoration, healing, and growth?

6. Is there an area of your life that God might be calling you to develop a mastery over, to retake control? How do you feel about this invitation? What might you gain if you pursue it?

Becoming a King: Session 5
The Way of Becoming

WATCH

As a group, watch Session 5

READ (Optional)

Chapters 7, 8, and 9 of *Becoming a King*

SHARE

Choose from the following questions to help guide your conversation.

1. What does the context of your life look like right now? What would the context need to look like for your masculine soul to thrive? How are these two worlds different?

2. Think about the last week: what are the most predictable habits in your life? Which of these habits are strengthening your process of becoming wholehearted and which ones are blocking growth and maturation?

3. What is your current relational model? What is the way you relate to people? Where do you invest your time, energy, and emotional resources?

4. Imagine you traveled five years down the road and you have become the kind of person who invests his time, money, and emotional capacity in a way that is healthy and strong for your soul. What would this more wholehearted and mature relational model for your life look like? How do this person and the person you are now differ?

5. What is the current pace of your life? How does it compare to the pace of your soul? Is this difference sustainable?

6. How do you respond to the idea that God is more interested in developing you as a man than he is in developing your personal kingdom? How might you redirect your energy and orient toward excavating yourself before building your kingdom?

Becoming a King: Session 6
Becoming a King

WATCH

As a group, watch Session 6

READ (Optional)

Chapter 10 of *Becoming a King*

SHARE

Choose from the following questions to help guide your conversation.

1. Jesus says, "Very truly I tell you, the Son can do nothing by himself; he can do only what he sees his Father doing" (John 5:19). Jesus' strength comes directly from dependency on the Father. Where and how do you see Jesus being dependent on the Father?

2. In comparison, do you find strength through dependency in your own life? If you were to be honest about your relationship with God, how would you describe it (think quality, frequency, and level of relating)?

3. Have you had an experience in your life where God needed to show up or all would be lost? What was that like?

4. Does your faith in God contain a deep dependency and reliance on moment-by-moment interaction with God? Why or why not? What if it did?

5. Who is the person that you would like to be in a decade? What is he like?

6. What will you specifically do to participate in the slow and steady process of *becoming* in order to be that man?

ADVENTURE TOGETHER

WEEK 24

Written into the core of the masculine soul is the need for adventure.

The danger and the wildness of it answers deep questions inside of us that the prefabricated world around us simply cannot answer. "Who am I?" and "What am I made of?" cannot be answered by the microwave, the mall, or your smartphone.

The heart needs to be in a landscape that matches the geography of the soul.

Remember the heroes of Scripture: Moses encountered God deep in the deserts of Sinai. Jacob's wrestling match with God took place in a wadi somewhere east of the Jabbok, in Mesopotamia, not on the living room floor.

John the Baptist and Elijah went to the wild to recover their strength. It was into the wilderness that the Spirit led Jesus. And it was from there that he received his identity.

If we are ever to learn who we are and why we're here, we must take that same journey.

Endless hours at the computer screen, meetings, and memos drive a man's heart into a dull resignation. But the soul cannot be harnessed. Our hearts will not take the shape of an alarm clock or email. As D. H. Lawrence said, "I am not a mechanism." We need connection with the earth and to feel something real in our hands—a shovel, a fly rod, the handlebars of a mountain bike.

Consider the difference between the experience of the last Star Wars movie or spy novel or blockbusting video game and your experience of a typical Bible study. How would you describe the contrast . . . and which makes your heart come alive more?

Adventure is deeply inscribed on the masculine heart.

But it is not just about having fun or going on vacation. Adventure tests us. It nourishes our souls by providing the answers we crave and need spoken to again and again. Adventure *requires* something of us. Though, to be honest, we fear the test, fear what it might say. What if I can't come through? What if I can't make it?

Exactly. What if?

Male friendships are forged when we must rely on the strength of others. Our relationship with God begins when we reach the end of ourselves. What need do we have for God in the comfort and safety of our controlled, tailored lives?

If a man says he doesn't want adventure, it is only because he doesn't know that he has what it takes. And the desire will play out in some other way—sports, Netflix, gambling, an affair, or a driven need for validation at work. We may fear what adventure will reveal, but we want to know what we are made of. The untested life is the unexamined life, ready to crumble at the slightest adversity.

We can't escape the simple fact that there is something wild in the masculine heart.

At some point in your year together, you will undertake an adventure. This does not mean you have to recreate an episode of Bear Grylls's *Man vs Wild*. Adventure is built into the core desires of your heart, but you do not need to put yourself in the most dangerous situation you can think of in order to act on that desire.

And yet it is when we overcome an entirely unexpected trial that we feel ourselves to be proven. Often, the best moments of an adventure are when things go wrong and we have to work together to make it through. But these moments are not necessarily frequent nor mandatory, and you do not need to fabricate them.

Our heart's need for adventure is met in the trials and tribulations of daily life. And it is met in the adventure of leaving our routines behind for a time. To get into wilderness—to get out of the fabricated worlds we live in—is adventure. Getting out there with other men feeds our desire for camaraderie and fellowship.

ADVENTURE IDEAS

There are endless options for your group's adventure. Here are just a few.

- Fly Fishing

The beauty of water, having a fly rod in your hand, paying intimate attention to what's around you, and the almost ludicrous hope to hold a fish in your hand. These are just a few of the joys of fly fishing.

A fly-fishing excursion can be an excellent way to spend your trip together. If one of your group members is an avid fly fisherman, then you have lucked out and can rely on his experience. But if this will be a new experience for everyone, it's well worth it to hire a guide for your first day out. Learning the basics from a professional will make the whole trip more rewarding and enjoyable.

You'll also need to determine which water is within reasonable distance to you and is good for fishing. Your local fly shop is your best friend in all of this. Ask where they recommend you go and which flies to use.

Yes there can be a bit of elitism in this community (as there is in almost every community of experts). But everyone was a beginner once, and the entire journey of the masculine soul is oriented around apprenticeship.

There is usually a place for tent camping around good water, but if that's not your thing, there may be cheap cabins for rent that cater to fly fishermen.

The following gear list is by no means exhaustive, but it can get you started. Much of the specialized gear can be rented.

What you'll need:

Gear

- ☐ Fly rod
- ☐ Reel
- ☐ Assorted flies
- ☐ Line Clippers
- ☐ Floatant
- ☐ Forceps
- ☐ Tippet
- ☐ A net (if the fish you're after are big enough)

Clothes

- ☐ Water shoes (Chacos/ Keens) or waders
- ☐ Quick dry shorts and/ or pants
- ☐ Quick dry shirt
- ☐ Hat
- ☐ Sunglasses
- ☐ Sunscreen

- **Backpacking**

Being in the mountains and the high country with nothing but what you carry is an incredible way to pursue adventure. It tests your ability to rough it while you make the journey to landscapes of exquisite beauty. The view from the top of a pass or the first look at an alpine bowl makes all the burning in your leg muscles worth it.

There are an infinite number of trails and you can tailor the distance and difficulty level of your hike. All you need is wilderness and a willingness to explore. Alltrails.com is a great resource for choosing routes.

The basic steps for undertaking a backpacking trip are pretty much the same as any adventure—research and proper planning—but there are a few unique aspects to consider.

There is no completely accurate weather forecast for the high country, so even if it predicts blue skies for the nearest town to your trailhead, you'll still want warm layers and rain gear. Part of your research will be to call the nearest forest ranger station to where you're going and ask about trail conditions and road closures. Many have had a trip stall out by a closed road Google Maps didn't know about.

Be extra vigilant about staying hydrated at higher altitudes. That starts with familiarizing yourself with how to keep properly hydrated and knowing the symptoms of altitude sickness. Your local REI or gear store may offer entry-level courses into first aid, essential items to pack, and how to read maps. They can also be a great resource to your trip planning.

What you'll need:

Group Gear

- ☐ Tent (rainfly, footprint, poles, stakes)
- ☐ Water purifier (and iodine)
- ☐ Camp chairs (i.e. Crazy Creek)
- ☐ Toilet paper
- ☐ Hand sanitizer
- ☐ Matches
- ☐ Lighter
- ☐ Med kit (with Ambien and extra Advil)
- ☐ Spare batteries
- ☐ Sunscreen
- ☐ Bug repellent
- ☐ Map (compass)

Kitchen

- ☐ Camp stove
- ☐ Fuel
- ☐ Pot(s)
- ☐ Utensils
- ☐ Bowls
- ☐ Mugs
- ☐ Snack bags
- ☐ Rope
- ☐ Knife
- ☐ Cooking oil
- ☐ Frying pan (optional)
- ☐ Spatula (optional)
- ☐ Dish soap
- ☐ Scrubber
- ☐ Kerchief (dish towel)
- ☐ Trash bag

Personal Gear

- ☐ Wool socks (1 + .5x number of days)
- ☐ Underwear (1 + .5x number of days)
- ☐ Wool base layer top
- ☐ Wool base layer bottom
- ☐ Hiking shorts, non-cotton
- ☐ Hiking shirt, non-cotton (1-2)
- ☐ Warm hat (wool is great)
- ☐ Ball cap (optional)
- ☐ Hiking pants, non-cotton (optional)
- ☐ Rain jacket
- ☐ Fleece or down jacket
- ☐ Mid-layer
- ☐ Rain pants (optional if wearing hiking pants)
- ☐ Hiking boots
- ☐ Camp shoes—something light, like Vans or Tevas (optional)
- ☐ Backpack (and rain cover)
- ☐ Headlamp
- ☐ Water bottles (2)
- ☐ Toothbrush and toothpaste

- ☐ Essential toiletries
  (meds, retainers, etc.)
- ☐ Travel deodorant
  (optional)
- ☐ Sleeping bag with stuff sack
- ☐ Sleeping pad
  (with patch kit)
- ☐ Trekking poles
- ☐ Pocket knife
- ☐ Hammock (optional)

- ☐ Sunglasses (optional)
- ☐ Chapstick
- ☐ Tobacco (optional)
- ☐ Whiskey (optional)
- ☐ Fly rod and flies (optional)
- ☐ Book (optional)
- ☐ Journal and pen
- ☐ Playing cards

MENU

Snacks

- ☐ Dried fruit
- ☐ Beef jerky
- ☐ Trail mix
- ☐ Bars
- ☐ Nut-butter pouches
- ☐ A treat (candy bars)

Lunch

- ☐ Salami
- ☐ Crackers
- ☐ Hard cheese
- ☐ Peanut butter and jelly
  tortilla wraps

Breakfast

- ☐ Dehydrated milk
  and granola
- ☐ Dehydrated eggs
  w/ bacon bits
- ☐ Hot sauce

Dinner

- ☐ Freeze-dried meals

- **Mountain Biking**

A mountain-biking trip combines the joys of car-camping with testing yourself against grueling climbs and heart pounding descents. For many years, we've headed to the desert of Moab, Utah, with a group of men for a week of mountain biking, rock climbing, and cigars around the campfire. There are excellent mountain-biking sites around the country. Find one near you, grab camping gear, and head out.

If you have never mountain biked before but would like to, there are beginners courses offered wherever there is mountain biking available, along with equipment rentals and mountain bike shops that can get you pointed in the right direction. REI is a great resource here as well.

Besides camping gear, you'll need:

- ☐ Mountain bike
- ☐ Bike helmet
- ☐ Tire patch kits
- ☐ Spare tubes
- ☐ Bike pump
- ☐ Day bag
- ☐ Trail food
- ☐ Water bottles/Camelbaks

Your group will figure out what it wants to do! Find something that matches the overall interests, physical abilities, and budgets of your guys. Then plan it and make the shared adventure a reality. Your soul will thank you for it!

LEADER'S CAIRN

So let's get practical. How do you pull off a trip into the wild landscapes our hearts were made for?

HOW TO PLAN YOUR ADVENTURE

We recommend taking this trip during the summer. This may fall at different points in your year with men, depending on when you started together.

We've already listed some ideas for possible adventures. You can go more ambitious (kayaking in the Sea of Cortés) or you can keep it simple (rent a forest service cabin nearby). The first step is deciding what to do and where best to do it. Here we'll cover the basics of how to plan the group trip. As mentioned in the first Leader's Cairn, you will want to make your plans well in advance.

First, determine what would be the best adventure for your group. For instance, if several men are not able to do a rigorous hike, then hiking isn't the right choice. It needs to be something everyone can do. This will help narrow down where to go and what's needed.

STEP 1: Research

Jump online and learn about what you want to go do. If your group of men wants to try something none of you has done before, consider using a guiding service or including some professional instruction on your first day.

Fully guided experiences get pricey fast, but getting a little instruction before you undertake something new is quite doable. Consider checking out the classes your local outdoor gear shop is offering. They have a wide offering of courses and curriculum at a modest budget.

Research the area. Where are you staying? What will the weather be like? What permits do you need? The gear you need to bring depends on the landscape and weather.

Again, if you're trying out something new, go for it, but do some research on what equipment you'll need. You may be able to rent or borrow much of what you need to keep costs down.

STEP 2: Make a Plan

When making a plan, think about the details from beginning to end. Account for the little minutiae of travel. How will you get there? Will you need accommodations along the way? What will you do for meals? How much will it cost per man?

Think through each day step by step and address logistics as they come up. This process will help create the detailed itinerary.

STEP 3: Delegate

As leader, you'll be spearheading the planning for your trip, but you are not the professional, paid guide. Delegate responsibility among the men in your group. Being in charge of something is part of the nourishment that comes through adventure.

This trip won't do much for the men if nothing is ever required of them. If they have experience, perhaps they can teach a portion of the adventure skills to other men. If they don't, it's an invitation to be initiated into something new.

TIME OFF

WEEKS 25–28

We all need time off for restoration and breathing easy. A chance to step away from the normal routine and replenish.

Ask God how best to fill this space. And then spend that time following his lead.

See you in four weeks!

UNIT #4

BAND OF BROTHERS

Weeks 29–38

INTRODUCTION TO
Band of Brothers

"But we in it shall be remembered—
We few, we happy few, we band of brothers;
For he today that sheds his blood with me
Shall be my brother" *Henry V* (IV, iii).

For this part of your year together, you will watch the HBO series *Band of Brothers*. It follows the legendary E Company, 2nd Battalion, 506th Parachute Infantry Regiment of the 101st Airborne Division through their experiences in World War II.

The series depicts heroism, sacrifice, and immense bravery in the face of insurmountable odds—men of competency with a mastery over their worlds.

After each episode, there are guided discussion questions to lead you into deeper conversation about what the scenes and themes stirred in you.

This is a depiction of war, however, so be warned there is intense language (the series is rated R) and some gory scenes that are hard to watch. We do not watch this series because it is violent. The graphic battle depictions in this series do not stir our hearts because they are violent. They stir our hearts because they speak to something at the core of who we are as men.

The story and scenes resonate because they empower us to face the many battles in our lives with courage. They remind us to step into our identity as a warrior. We as men were made in the image of God, and God is undoubtedly a warrior: "The LORD is a warrior; the LORD is his name" (Ex. 15:3). Deep within who we are, in our identity as men, is the desire to live out our God-given identity as a warrior. This is obvious in young boys who will make a weapon out of anything—a pistol out of a graham cracker, a sword out of a stick.

May this series of battle, heroism, and sacrifice stir your heart as it speaks to key pieces of your identity and who God is calling you to be. There's something far larger at play here. Though imperfect, *Band of Brothers* offers a powerful metaphor for what we do in service of the kingdom of God and for the fellowship as men we are called to in the midst of a world at war.

LEADER'S CAIRN

For this unit, you will spend each session together watching one episode from *Band of Brothers*. Go to WildatHeart.org/AYearwithMen for various ways to purchase this series. After each week's episode, use the discussion questions to lead men into deeper conversation.

These episodes are longer than the videos from previous units. The shortest is 52 minutes and the longest is an hour and thirteen minutes. You'll need to plan accordingly to have adequate time to watch and discuss each episode. If you have never seen the miniseries before, it would be a good idea to watch it before the group does. This is helpful so you will not be surprised by the events of each episode, to determine if you need to skip a particular scene, and so you can understand the questions before your group meets.

There are more questions per episode than there will be time to answer. As you know by now, you do not need every question to fill your time together. Familiarize yourself with *Band of Brothers* and try to select the questions you feel will be most beneficial to your group of men.

Band of Brothers: Episode 1
Currahee

WATCH

As a group, watch Episode 1

SHARE

Choose from the following questions to help guide your conversation.

Initiation

- At the beginning, we meet the men as they are preparing for the invasion of Normandy, before returning to their days of training. There is a level of competency that is only attained through years of grueling work. Does this image align with how you picture your own growth, development, and initiation?

- Does watching these men prepare to invade Normandy, "the Great Crusade, toward which we have striven these many months," stir a sense of longing for a clear mission, with everything on the line, shared with a tightly knit group of men with whom you've developed a hard-earned competency? Share why.

- What areas of your life are calling you to sacrifice? Do you feel equipped to do so?

Leadership

"Never put yourself in a position where you can take from these men."
—Lt. Winters

This episode presents two very different depictions of leadership, that of Capt. Sobel and that of Lt. Winters.

- How would you describe the leadership of Capt. Sobel? Does he command respect?

- How would you describe the leadership of Lt. Winters? How does he earn the respect of his men?

- When Capt. Sobel punishes the entire company for the inflated infractions of the few, does it frustrate you? Why?

Camaraderie

> "These men have been through the toughest training the army has to offer under the worst possible circumstances. And they volunteered for it. You know why they volunteered? So when things got really bad, the man in the foxhole next to them would be the best." —Lt. Winters

> "Once we get into combat, the only person you can trust is yourself, and the fella next to you." —Sgt. Guarnere

- When Pvt. "Smokey" Gordon is singled out by Capt. Sobel to run Mt. Currahee by himself, he is joined by three other men who run with him even though they do not have to. They subvert the isolation imposed by Capt. Sobel. What did this scene stir in you?

- In what ways does this depict camaraderie and male friendship?

- An unbreakable bond is forged through suffering together when you realize your own limits and you have to rely on someone else to make it through. That is where male bonds and friendships are forged. How do the bonds between the men of Easy Company compare to your own friendships?

Depictions of Masculinity

> "You're making me look bad, Lieutenant." —Capt. Sobel

- Does Capt. Sobel display authentic masculinity? What does he portray?

- How does Capt. Sobel handle making mistakes and being wrong?

- In what ways is Capt. Sobel a poser?

- How does Lt. Winters compare to Capt. Sobel? What kind of masculinity does Lt. Winters display?

Band of Brothers: Episode 2
Day of Days

WATCH

As a group, watch Episode 2

SHARE

Choose from the following questions to help guide your conversation.

Masculinity

- As the series continues and characters are developed, we see different depictions of masculinity, both good and bad. Sgt. Guarnere plays a large role in this episode. What kind of masculinity does he portray?

- How does Sgt. Guarnere make decisions? What is motivating Sgt. Guarnere?

- At the end of Easy Company's first engagement with the enemy, Lt. Winters loses his first man. How does he handle it? What does this say about Lt. Winters as a leader?

- How does Lt. Winters continue to gain the respect of his men?

- Who are you identifying with most in this episode?

Courage

- Jumping from the plane while under intense fire, the men move toward their objective. Despite being scattered in the dark, Lt. Winters and his ragtag group of Easy Company men take on the German gun encampment. What do these depictions of courage stir in you?

- "Courage" comes from the Latin word *cor* meaning "heart," and the Anglo-French word *corage* meaning the heart as "the seat of emotions." "Core," as in the core of who you are, also comes from the Latin word for "heart." Courage is central to who we are. Share an example when you displayed courage—or a time you wish you had.

- What are the motivations driving these men to be courageous? Are you identifying with their motivations?

The Call to Be a Warrior

Remember, the depictions of battle in this series do not stir our hearts because they are violent. They stir our hearts because they speak to something at the core of who we as men are meant to be: warriors.

- What do the battle scenes stir in you?

- What battles are you facing in your life right now—and what are they demanding of you?

- The conflict to overtake the German gun embattlement is exemplary. The stakes are high and the danger is real. There are only 12 men to overtake an encampment of roughly 60. It is not just that men desire to be a part of a battle, but a battle that deeply matters, where we each have a crucial role to play. What does this bring up in you?

Band of Brothers: Episode 3
Carentan

WATCH

As a group, watch Episode 3

SHARE

Choose from the following questions to help guide your conversation.

Courage in the Face of Fear

> "I think everybody had fear. I think there's people that can handle fear."
> —Pvt. Tipper

> "Courage is not the absence of fear, but rather the assessment that something else is more important than fear." —Franklin D. Roosevelt

- The men of Easy Company put their lives on the line to deliver Normandy from the occupation of Nazi Germany. The soldiers face their fear of pain and death in a variety of ways. How do some men overcome their fear? How do others not?

- Pvt. Blithe suffers from "Hysterical Blindness," a psychiatric condition where one goes temporarily blind from trauma or severe stress. Can you identify in some ways with Blithe?

- 1st platoon of Easy Company comes under fire while approaching the town of Carentan, and their first instinct is to duck for cover in the ditches. Yet the only way to safety is to move into the fire. How does Lt. Winters demonstrate courage in the midst of this situation? What is most important to Lt. Winters?

- Lt. Harry Welsh tells Pvt. Blithe, "It's a game, Blithe. That's all. Hell, we're just moving the ball forward one yard at a time. Nothing but a game." How is Lt. Welsh handling his fear?

Sacrifice

> "There is no greater love than to lay down one's life for one's friends"
> (John 15:13 NLT).

- Lt. Welsh rushes the machine gun encampment in Carentan to get a grenade through the window. Lt. Welsh and McGrath, the rocketeer, fire on the oncoming tanks while they are exposed in the middle of the field. How do these moments of sacrifice and bravery speak to you?

- We witness moments of courageous action paralleled with moments of restraint, such as when Sgt. Luz decides not to throw a grenade into a building only to discover a family of civilians taking cover there. What stands out to you about his decision?

- At the end of this episode, we see TSgt. Malarkey picking up the laundry and hearing all the names of those who didn't make it back. Sixty-five men have lost their lives in the 23 days of combat on the front lines. How do you process such loss? What do you do with Pvt. Blithe's death?

Initiation

> "That's Edelweiss. That only grows in the Alps above the tree line. Which means he climbed up there to get it. It's supposed to be the mark of a true soldier." —Capt. Nixon

- While waiting for the coming battle, Lt. Speirs says to Blithe, "The only hope you have to accept is that you're already dead. And as soon as you accept that the sooner you'll be able to function as a soldier's supposed to function—without mercy, without compassion, without remorse. All war depends upon it." How does Lt. Speirs view the process of initiation to become a soldier?

- How does Lt. Winters' view of initiation differ?

- What is required to be initiated? Who performs the initiation and what are its effects?

- Can you identify with Pvt. Blithe's process of initiation? Why or why not?

- How are the Purple Hearts and the Edelweiss similar?

Band of Brothers: Episode 4
Replacements

WATCH

As a group, watch Episode 4

SHARE

Choose from the following questions to help guide your conversation.

Belonging

> "The Toccoa men, that's the ones that was there at the very beginning, they are very close. They accept people coming in like myself as a replacement, but you also had to prove yourself." —Don King

- Pvt. Cobb makes replacement Pvt. Miller take off the Presidential Distinguished Unit Citation awarded to the Company for its service in Normandy because he joined the regiment after Normandy. We quickly learn that Pvt. Cobb didn't fight in Normandy either because he was wounded on the plane. How is Pvt. Cobb posing?

- Does Pvt. Cobb feel like an initiated man in this scene?

- Does Pvt. Cobb seem to be secure or insecure in his identity as a member of the unit?

Initiation

- At the battle of Nuenen, the replacements fight their first battle. How does this compare to the first days of fighting in Normandy?

- Pvt. Miller is killed in combat during the fighting at Nuenen. How do you view Pvt. Cobb's actions toward Pvt. Miller after he loses his life?

- Initiation is performed by already initiated men. For the replacements, this is often performed by Sgt. "Bull" Randleman, who offers the kind of advice that only comes from experience. Do you have a figure like this in your life?

- Give an example of how you've been—or not been—initiated as a man. What impact has that had on you?

Defeat

"I never fired a shot, the whole time." —Pvt. Hashey

- Operation Market Garden took a great deal of risk . . . and it failed. Easy Company's regiment lost 180 men while 560 were injured. This is their first defeat. How do you think the men are feeling as they retreat?

- How do you think the men are feeling, especially SSgt. Martin as he withdraws without knowing where Bull is?

- How do you think the replacements are feeling after their first battle where they lose so many comrades?

- Loss of life is always tragic . . . but there are also many other kinds of loss. What loss has had the greatest impact on you? Why?

Band of Brothers: Episode 5
Crossroads

WATCH

As a group, watch Episode 5

SHARE

Choose from the following questions to help guide your conversation.

Leadership

> "If you're a leader, you lead the way. Not just on the easy ones, you take the tough ones, too." —Capt. Winters

> "He went right in there and he didn't know. He never thought of not being first or sending somebody in his place. I don't know how he survived, but he did." —Pvt. "Popeye" Wynn

- We have seen the men make choices of incredible sacrifice, but leadership requires an even greater sacrifice: To not ask anyone to do something that you would not do yourself, to step into the line of fire first, to say, "Send me." This is exemplified when Capt. Winters moves ahead to scout the MG-42 gun encampment, as well as when he runs the field while his company waits for the smoke signal to advance. What do these depictions of leadership illustrate to you?

- In what areas of your life are you being asked to take the lead? To push into a frontier where you have never been, perhaps in a relationship, in your work, or in your spiritual life?

- Leaders often experience loneliness. Give an example of when you've found yourself alone through hard choices or to pave an uncharted path. What happened?

Competency

> *2nd Lt. George Rice:* "Looks like you guys are going to be surrounded."
>
> *Capt. Winters:* "We're paratroopers, Lieutenant. We're supposed to be surrounded."

- We have seen the men of Easy Company demonstrate a remarkable level of competency. Knowing exactly what to do and when to do it. We get a sense of the 101st Airborne's elite nature when they are called in to replace the 4th Army at Bastogne. Do you feel like you have this level of competency when a crisis happens and life goes sideways?

- What might you do to gain more competency in your life?

> *1st Lt. Walsh:* "We didn't know what to do."
>
> *Cpl. Roe (medic):* "Yeah, well, you oughta. You know, you are officers, you are grown-ups. You oughta know."

- These men who exhibit such confidence and competency have moments where they are completely at a loss as to what to do. When Lt. "Moose" Heyliger is wounded by friendly fire, Lt. Welsh does not follow protocol while administering morphine syringes. How do you handle making a mistake?

- What do mistakes, some of them life-threatening, say about these men?

- What do you believe mistakes say about you?

Identity

> "Keep moving and lead the way." —Capt. Winters

- How is Capt. Winters feeling about his promotion to executive officer of the battalion? His leadership and tactics are unquestionable, and they need him in command, but he must leave the men he has trained with, fought with, and risked his life for. For many men, their motivation to fight is to keep the man in the foxhole next to him alive. What is Capt. Winters's motivation?

- Can you identify with Capt. Winters? Why or why not?

- Capt. Winters must let go of the men he has risked his life for and give direct leadership over to someone else. By doing so, how has Winters's sense of identity shifted? How has his capacity as a leader, and therefore his leadership, shifted because of this?

> "A good leader has to understand the people that are under him."
> —Lt. "Buck" Compton

- How do you imagine the men of Easy Company feel about their new commanding officer, Lt. Dike, being a replacement who has not gone through what they have?

Band of Brothers: Episode 6
Bastogne

WATCH

As a group, watch Episode 6

SHARE

Choose from the following questions to help guide your conversation.

The next two episodes contain several scenes that are particularly graphic. We don't watch depictions of war because we enjoy gore and violence. Far from it. We watch because in war the stakes are the highest they can possibly be: life and death, victory or defeat. We watch because those stakes contain a clarity that our normal daily trials do not. We watch to see demonstrations of valor, heroism, sacrifice, and courage in the face of terrible odds that we might demonstrate similar attributes in our own lives.

Bravery

In this episode, we follow one of Easy Company's medics, Cpl. Eugene Roe. Cpl. Roe is faced with dire circumstances and insurmountable odds. The 101st Airborne division is completely surrounded by German forces during the Battle of the Bulge. The company is under sporadic artillery fire, has no aid station or winter clothes, and is low on food and ammunition. Cpl. Roe has no plasma, a couple of bandages, little to no morphine, and scrounges what he can from personal aid kits. It is under these circumstances that he must do what he can to save the lives of his comrades.

- What comes up in you when you watch Cpl. Roe face these odds and commit himself to trying to save as many lives as possible?

- When have you faced insurmountable odds? What did you do . . . and what did it cost you?

- Cpl. Roe's bravery is unquestioned. When a wounded soldier cries "Medic!" he runs toward the call through the German artillery fire—conditions in which no other man dares to leave his foxhole. What does his courage stir in you?

Selflessness

> "Oh Lord, grant that I shall never seek so much to be consoled
> as to console, to be understood as to understand,
> or to be loved as to love with all my heart, with all my heart."
> —Cpl. Roe, from the "Prayer of St. Francis"

- Cpl. Roe demonstrates radical selflessness: He gives what supplies he is able to scrounge up to the other medic in the unit and sends him away from the front line to get a hot meal instead of himself. When the soldier watching the line loses his boots, Cpl. Roe takes it upon himself to find him new boots. While freezing in his own foxhole, Cpl. Roe brings other soldiers a blanket. Besides healing the wounded, Cpl. Roe, the medic, is the man that takes care of everyone else. What does this selflessness stir in you? Is there something about it that feels impossible?

- Who in your life has sacrificed the most for you? How?

- Is this kind of selflessness something you aspire to? Why or why not?

- What areas of your life in this season require greater selflessness?

Cost

> "I never want to treat a wounded man again. I'd rather work in a butcher shop." —Renee

We see the emotional cost of sacrifice. Cpl. Roe offers his rare chocolate to Pvt. "Babe" Heffron to try and ease his emotional suffering when he is unable to save his friend. We also see it after the members of the disastrous patrol return and Capt. Winters simply sits with his men, using the power of presence where words fail. Toward the end of the episode, Cpl. Roe himself is clearly suffering from traumatic stress. He is overwhelmed by the task of trying to save lives in war with so few resources.

- What have the battles in your life cost you?

- Are there areas in your life where you should be sacrificing less? Why or why not?

- Despite this cost, no member of the 101st ever agreed that the division needed to be rescued. What gave the men the confidence to continue on and believe that they could win?

Band of Brothers: Episode 7
The Breaking Point

WATCH

As a group, watch Episode 7

SHARE

Choose from the following questions to help guide your conversation.

Leadership

> "Dike wasn't a bad leader because he made bad decisions.
> He was a bad leader because he made no decisions." —Sgt. Lipton

Finding a competent leader for Easy Company in the midst of loss and suffering proves difficult for Capt. Winters—especially someone decisive who commands the respect of his men. The clear choice is Lt. "Buck" Compton, but he has changed since being wounded in Holland. So the company is stuck with the disastrously incompetent Lt. Dike.

- What impact does Lt. Dike's incompetence have on the men?

- How do you handle an incompetent leader?

- Besides putting the lives of others at risk, why is an incompetent leader so frustrating?

Sgt. Lipton fills the gap in leadership by keeping track of who is wounded, delivering the news of Cpl. Hoobler's death to Capt. Winters, maintaining the morale of the men, and making good tactical decisions.

- In what ways do you identify with Sgt. Lipton?

- Would you follow him? Why or why not?

- What is your main takeaway about leadership from this episode?

Lt. Dike's toxic leadership culminates in his disastrous charge across the field to the town of Foy. His incompetence is juxtaposed with that of Capt. Speirs, who comes in to relieve him, salvages the operation, and takes the town of Foy.

- How does Lt. Dike demonstrate inauthentic masculinity and posing?

- How does Capt. Speirs demonstrate authentic masculinity?

- Has there been a person in your life who came into a dire situation, and, with decisiveness and competency, turned things around? Share that story and why it mattered.

Fear

> "Fear is poison in combat. It's something we all felt, but you just didn't show it. You can't. It's destructive and it's contagious." —Sgt. Lipton

- What do you do with fear? Not just the fear of being in a dangerous situation, but the fear that comes with everyday life: the fear of failure, a difficult conversation, loss, the future, your finances, etc.

- Capt. Speirs demonstrates remarkable courage when he runs through the German lines to complete his mission. What does his bravery stir in you?

- Another moment of courage is demonstrated by Sgt. Lipton running the field so the marksman SSgt. "Shifty" Powers can get a shot off at the German sniper. How does acting with courage inspire others to act with courage?

Bonding Through Suffering

> "I'm not sure that anybody who lived through that one hasn't carried with him, in some hidden ways, the scars. Perhaps that is the factor that helps keep Easy men bonded so unusually close together."
> —Capt. Winters

We see Sgt. Muck give a roster of the company's wounds to the new replacement. Everyone but a few has been wounded in some way or another. There is a camaraderie of mutual suffering. Fellowships have been forged in the fire of war. Male bonds are not forged through small talk. They are forged through suffering together during transformative experiences. This isn't to say only bad circumstances create lasting friendships, but that hard times and costly victories do create a shared solidarity in those who go through it together. This is how a band of brothers is forged.

- Despite the unforgiving conditions and the brutality of war, no one wants to leave—Sgt. Toye returns early from the hospital and TSgt. Malarkey turns down the offer to be Capt. Winters's runner for a few days. What motivates them to stay?

- How can you enter into the suffering of the men in your group?

- What would it look like to live in a fellowship based on a common mission where you share each other's battles? How might being a part of something like this change your life?

Band of Brothers: Episode 8
The Last Patrol

WATCH

As a group, watch Episode 8

SHARE

Choose from the following questions to help guide your conversation.

Earning Your Seat at the Table

> "Must've liked that hospital, 'cause we left Holland four months ago . . .
> Well I'm sure you tried to bust out and help us in Bastogne, Web . . .
> Popeye found a way, so did Alley, right, back in Holland. And Guarnere—"
> —Cpl. Liebgott

- What are the men feeling as they leave Belgium?

- Can you identify with the men who treat Pvt. Webster as a replacement?

- Can you identify with Pvt. Webster, who feels like he must re-earn his place?

- Do you feel like you need to constantly earn your seat at the table? Why or why not?

Experience

> "Getting back safely could be successfully accomplished in as little as
> ten minutes. The same mission could be met with disaster and result
> in nothing more than fifteen Americans killed or wounded in action.
> Those of us who had seen combat before put that out of our minds.
> Those who hadn't probably thought of little else as we waited for
> darkness." —Pvt. Webster

- The difference between the men who have been seasoned by combat and the replacements or non-combat servicemen is abundantly clear. How has the experience of war changed the men?

- TSgt. Malarkey has been on the front lines every time Easy Company has been deployed into combat since the invasion of Normandy, whereas Lt. Jones has just arrived. Describe the contrast between these two men.

- Lt. Jones is turned down to lead the patrol because he doesn't have any experience. What is motivating him to see combat? Can you identify with that longing?

- Do you typically avoid opportunities where you don't have experience … or choose to enter into them as a way to gain experience? How does that approach tend to work for you?

Knowing Your Stories

"I wondered if people back home would ever know what it cost the soldiers to win this war … How could anyone ever know of the price paid by soldiers in terror, agony, and bloodshed if they'd never been to places like Normandy, Bastogne, or Haguenau?" —Pvt. Webster

- The only ones who can fully know what a situation was like are the people who were there. This is why it is important to have witnesses to your story. Do you have witnesses to your story? How is that helpful?

- Even if we have witnesses to some events, we all have moments of courage and sacrifice that no one sees. What do you do with those moments?

Band of Brothers: Episode 9
Why We Fight

WATCH

As a group, watch Episode 9

SHARE

Choose from the following questions to help guide your conversation.

Justice

> "A lot of those soldiers, I've thought about this often, that man and I might have been good friends. We might have had a lot in common ... Of course, they were doing what they were supposed to do, and I was trying to do what I was supposed to do." —SSgt. "Shifty" Powers

- The title of this episode is *Why We Fight*. We have seen different answers, such as in the first attempt to liberate Holland, when Pvt. Webster provides a boy with his first taste of chocolate. For some men, it is the liberation of a people. For others, it is just the right thing to do. While on the truck, Pvt. Janovec is reading an article that says "the Germans are bad." An obvious remark to the soldiers who have seen their friends killed in action, but also a vague and nonspecific sentiment toward the enemy. What changes for the men when they see the concentration camp?

- How does the experience of the concentration camp change their understanding of the war and their motivations for fighting it?

- Is it hard to comprehend that people are capable of such evil? Why or why not?

- As the men enter Germany, a sign reads, "You are now entering enemy territory. Keep on the alert." It serves as a wake-up call to prevent the men from lowering their guard. What do you use as a reminder or wake-up call that you live in a world at war?

Masculinity and Emotion

> *Maj. Winters:* "You tell 'em what you always tell 'em: Their sons died as heroes."
>
> *Capt. Nixon:* "You really still believe that?"
>
> *Maj. Winters:* "Yeah. Yeah, I do. Don't you?"

- Does Capt. Nixon feel like an initiated man who has been tested? Why or why not?

- How does Capt. Nixon deal with the loss of the men in his plane?

- How does Maj. Winters deal with his grief and loss differently?

- What does how we handle our pain say about us?

Experience

- Why is Sgt. Perconte so angry at the new replacement?

- How does Pvt. O'Keefe compare to the other men? How do the other men treat his inexperience?

- What role does experience and initiation play in true masculinity?

Band of Brothers: Episode 10
Points

WATCH

As a group, watch Episode 10

SHARE

Choose from the following questions to help guide your conversation.

Finding Your Place

> "You thought that you could do just about anything after the war was over and you came back out. Well, you lost a lot of that, or at least I did. I lost all that confidence." —SSgt. "Shifty" Powers

- Are you surprised by Shifty's statement? Why or why not?

- Why do you think Shifty lost his confidence?

- Think about your own story. Why do some experiences fill you with confidence in the moment but don't last while other victories stay with you and provide strength to face future situations? Is it just a state of mind or is something more at play?

Fellowship

> "You've found in one another a bond that exists only in combat. Among brothers who've shared foxholes, held each other in dire moments, who've seen death and suffered together."
> —German general

- By the end of the war, the men have established an unbreakable bond with one another from fighting and suffering together. Despite being tragic, the fury of the drunk soldier shooting Sgt. Grant is elicited because of a fierce protectiveness for one another. What does this bond stir in you?

- SSgt. Talbert chooses to demote himself and take a lower rank so that he is not separated from the regular men. Can you identify with his decision?

- Capt. Speirs decides to stay with Easy Company despite having enough points to be demobilized. Why did he make this choice?

Reward

"'Were you a hero?' 'No, but I served in a company of heroes.'"
—Maj. Winters, remembering a letter from Sgt. Ranney

- How have these men changed over the course of the war?

- For comparison, what kind of man does the German colonel who surrendered to Maj. Winters seem to be?

- At the end, Capt. Sobel reappears. How does his childish attitude and shallow masculinity come across now, after the events of the war?

- These men who've endured unimaginable suffering with such indescribable courage go home to their ordinary lives. What do you make of their ending? What would be a just end for these men?

GET OUT AND DO

WEEK 39

With the completion of our last unit, this is a week to do something active as a group. If you're looking for ideas, check out the list provided in Week 8.

There's no pressure for this to be amazing. It's just a chance to enjoy time together around an activity.

Make it fun!

UNIT #5

FATHERED BY GOD

Weeks 40–47

INTRODUCTION TO
Fathered by God
BY JOHN ELDREDGE

Driving into the Colorado wilderness to look for the last fly fishing of the season, my friend relayed to me his most recent wrestling match with his car: "The mechanic told me it'd cost $500 to fix. But after looking online, I ordered a $5 part and got it running."

I did not feel the urge to celebrate with him.

In fact, the only things I felt were shame and embarrassment and the desperate need to change the subject. *I just had the mechanic fix my burnt-out headlight.*

Several days before, while getting ready for this very excursion, I had turned my attention to the burnt-out headlight that I had been ignoring for weeks. I read the manual, had the awkward interaction at AutoZone where the seasoned man behind the counter told me what I needed, and watched several YouTube videos. I walked out to my car armed with information, a screwdriver, and wobbling confidence. After several hours I had accomplished nothing except breaking one of the plastic rivets that keeps the wheel well on.

My friend had noticed my burnt out headlight and had offered to help me replace it. I had declined. I dreaded the feeling of looking like an idiot in front of another man; I preferred looking like an idiot in private.

Now as we meandered through dark timber on a backcountry road, I knew I would never let it slip that I had failed on my own and took it into a shop, especially after I denied his offer to help.

But I am not alone in this feeling.

In fact, that very friend had turned to the internet for help, too, and his success was largely due to the relative simplicity of the problem. But why did I feel so emasculated for not knowing how to do something I was never taught and had never done before?

How did you feel the last time you walked into Home Depot? Or when your washing machine began leaking? Or if that is your arena, how did you feel when you walked into your last meeting with your financial advisor, or spoke to your insurance agent to try and make a claim?

The men in our world and the world in which we live are both missing the vital capstone of the masculine journey.

As we discussed in *Wild at Heart*, masculinity is bestowed, and bestowed by the father. But we are in too many ways without a father. We live in a time of fatherlessness.

Most boys and most men do not have the kind of relationship with their fathers where the father guides them through the masculine journey. Our fathers are wounded and broken people and were not equipped, for many reasons, to offer the fathering we needed and still need.

We are unfathered men and therefore we are unfinished men.

We are boys in men's bodies.

Our way of looking at Christianity, at discipleship, leaves no room for God the Father. We do not have a father-view of the world, a view centered on the deep reality of the loving and strong presence of a father who is deeply engaged in our lives and journey, a father to turn to, a father who offers guidance and provision.

Consider this a relief: The life you have lived and known as a man is not all that life has to offer.

There is another path to walk, an ancient path paved for centuries by the men who have walked before us. A path marked with guideposts for us to follow.

There is a Father who deeply desires to give us the fathering we missed and deeply need. A Father who is committed to our wholeheartedness and our cultivation into the men we were meant to be, the men he has called us to be.

The following video session adapted from *Fathered by God* will lead you through the stages of the masculine journey and offer guideposts to receiving the fathering we desperately need from our true Father, not as a one-stop shop, but as an identity and as a way of life.

LEADER'S CAIRN

For this part of your year together, you will take your men through the *Fathered by God* video series.

As with previous units, each week your group will watch an episode and then use the following questions to facilitate the conversation. You'll want to determine in advance if you'd like the men to read the chapters of the book, *Fathered by God*. If so, they'll need time to purchase and read the chapters that relate to each session.

You can access this series for free at WildatHeart.org/AYearwithMen.

Fathered by God: Session 1
The Masculine Journey

WATCH

As a group, watch Session 1

READ (Optional)

Chapters 1 and 2 of *Fathered by God*

SHARE

Choose from the following questions to help guide your conversation.

1. When you were growing up, who modeled masculinity for you? Where did you turn to learn masculinity?

2. Who represents masculinity best in your world today? Why?

3. Each of us has been in a situation where we felt like we were fumbling for what to do because we'd never been taught how to do it. Share a memory of when you felt "unfathered."

4. Becoming a man is a process, and we've all missed key pieces of that journey. What did you not receive as a boy or young man? What does that reality bring up in you?

5. What is your internal reaction to the idea that God actually *wants* to father you?

6. God desires to initiate and father us through the hard seasons of life. What trial are you currently facing—and how open are you to letting God father you through it?

Fathered by God: Session 2
Boyhood

WATCH

As a group, watch Session 2

READ (Optional)

Chapter 3 of *Fathered by God*

SHARE

Choose from the following questions to help guide your conversation.

1. Our boyhood years are filled with discovery and adventure, from sword fighting with sticks to sports to learning an instrument to debate team. What is one of your favorite experiences of adventure as a boy? If nothing comes to mind, how are you feeling?

2. What does the term "beloved son" raise in you? Do you feel like the beloved son to your earthly dad?

3. If you are honest with yourself, how much do you really expect for God to be a father to you? Do you expect him to show up every day? Not at all?

4. For most of us, if not all, boyhood ends before it should. How was your boyhood stage ended prematurely?

5. It may be that you associate the failures of your earthly father with God as Father. Despite your father's failures (or even his successes), do you think God is truly a Father who cares about you and wants to give you good gifts?

6. No matter what life stage you are in now, you can still receive the fathering you missed in your boyhood stage. What are the ways you'd like to receive the joys of boyhood back into your heart?

Fathered by God: Session 3
Cowboy

WATCH

As a group, watch Session 3

READ (Optional)

Chapter 4 of *Fathered by God*

SHARE

Choose from the following questions to help guide your conversation.

1. While you were still in the cowboy stage, what was life's primary message to you?

2. Do you have memorable moments of adventure or hard work in your life that demanded more of you than you thought you had to offer? How did it go?

3. Was your cowboy stage cut short? In what ways was your heart wounded during your cowboy years?

4. Did your parents or guardians or mentors let you risk or experience hard work? If not, how has that affected you?

5. What do you do with the idea that God might invite you, as he did David, into great adventure and great danger?

6. What new adventures or opportunities for hard work could you enter into now that would invite God to father your cowboy heart? What does that stir in you?

Fathered by God: Session 4
Warrior

WATCH

As a group, watch Session 4

READ (Optional)

Chapter 5 of *Fathered by God*

SHARE

Choose from the following questions to help guide your conversation.

1. As a young boy, did you ever get into a fight? What were you fighting over and with whom were you fighting? How did it go?

2. Is God's identity as a warrior comforting or frightening to you? What does the warrior heart of God raise in you?

3. What have you tried to fight for in your life that didn't go well? What happened?

4. God is a warrior because there are things in this world that must be fought for. He placed a warrior's heart in you, in his own image, because there are things in your life you must fight for. In what part of your life are you being called up as a warrior?

5. What is your gut reaction to the battles in your life? Are you passive or driven? How so?

6. As a warrior, there are different ways to protect and fight for the hearts of those you love. How has prayer been a part of your arsenal?

Fathered by God: Session 5
Lover

WATCH

As a group, watch Session 5

READ (Optional)

Chapter 6 of *Fathered by God*

SHARE

Choose from the following questions to help guide your conversation.

1. Each of us leaves our boyhood behind when we recognize exquisite beauty. Who was the girl that awakened your heart to the beauty and romance of life? What did you learn about life from that experience?

2. When you experience natural beauty—perhaps a sunset, mountain, or crashing waves—what is your reaction? Has beauty ever stirred your heart toward God?

3. Do you engage with beauty or are you closed off? Do you hide behind logic and reason, as most of us do, or do you feel permission to engage with beauty and let it in?

4. Do you long for a more intimate relationship with God or does that make you uncomfortable? Why?

5. Your heart needs beauty. Where are you turning to find beauty in your life? Where might you better turn?

6. Do you feel nervous or unqualified to love a woman and care for her heart? Why or why not?

Fathered by God: Session 6
King

WATCH

As a group, watch Session 6

READ (Optional)

Chapter 7 of *Fathered by God*

SHARE

Choose from the following questions to help guide your conversation.

1. What king from history, literature, or myth do you like the most? What about this figure resonates with you?

2. How would you describe the kind of king you would like to be? What draws you to those traits?

3. How have you been initiated to handle power throughout your story? How have you *not* been initiated?

4. Right now, do you feel like God can entrust you with more power? If he did, what would you do with it?

5. How would others describe the kind of king you are becoming, especially those under your authority?

6. What habits and practices do you need to spend time in now to help make you the kind of king that God is inviting you to be?

Fathered by God: Session 7
Sage

WATCH

As a group, watch Session 7

READ (Optional)

Chapter 8 of *Fathered by God*

SHARE

Choose from the following questions to help guide your conversation.

1. A sage is someone who offers hard-earned wisdom as well as encouragement. Who in your life has been a sage to you? What has their impact been in your life?

2. Is a sage someone whom you desire to have in your life? Where could a sage speak into that would be most helpful? Your relationships? Your walk with God? Your finances?

3. If there has been a marked absence of sages in your life, have you considered approaching someone older or wiser for guidance? What does the thought of reaching out to them stir in you?

4. Do you look to God as a sage with your questions? Why or why not?

5. How do you feel about the process of becoming a sage? Can you accept that the only way to become a sage is through time and experience?

6. In what areas would you most like others to see you as a sage (either now or in the future)? Why?

Fathered by God: Session 8
Let Us Be Intentional

WATCH

As a group, watch Session 8

READ (Optional)

Chapter 9 of *Fathered by God*

SHARE

Choose from the following questions to help guide your conversation.

1. How has this study changed your understanding of what it means to be fathered by God?

2. Which stage of masculinity do you feel you need to spend more time in? Why?

3. What qualities of your earthly father do you need to let go of in order to see God the Father more clearly? How do you plan on doing that?

4. There is a huge difference between being intentional and striving. How would you describe it? In your own life, how do you see this difference playing out?

5. As you have gone through this series, has your understanding and desire for intimacy with God changed? How?

6. We all need further initiation. What will you do to actively seek it now?

CELEBRATE

WEEK 48

Congratulations! You've reached the summit of a rare journey that few men ever experience.

In this final week, take time to look back at the past year. Consider the new ways you've come to know God—and your story. Recall the shared adventures you've had with the men in your group.

Your leader will provide more details on what this last gathering will include. Perhaps it will take place at a favorite hangout rather than the usual meeting space.

But don't end with a whimper. Make this a time of rich, joyful celebration for all that's taken place. And all that's yet to come in each of your stories with God . . . and each other.

LEADER'S CAIRN

Make your last weekly meeting a celebration! Your group has just completed a year of study, conversation, fellowship, and adventure together. That's a rare accomplishment in this world of distraction and change.

Many groups will wrap up after this last time together. But if your group would like to continue, we've included a final section at the end of this book that lists other studies from *Wild at Heart*. It offers suggestions for your group once you finish your year, should you want to keep going.

For now, plan ahead on how to make this last gathering a celebration.

Here are a few suggestions for what to include:

- Recognize the significant journey each man has made
- Discuss highlights of the year
- Consecrate the year that has been to God
- Release the men with a blessing

Finish well.

You and the men in your group have achieved an amazing milestone!

NEW FRONTIER

You are finished with your year together. Now what?

The good news is that *there is so much more.*

Friends, we have but touched the tip of the iceberg. Discipleship is a life-long process. The work of the soul is done slowly. Even a year is a blink when it comes to this journey.

The spiritual life is always a frontier. So ask God what he has next for you.

If the content of a particular unit spoke to you, there is more. If you are still wrestling with certain concepts and ideas, there is more. Get the book. Get the workbook. Spend time going deeper into that particular message.

Consider going through Wild at Heart BASIC. This is Wild at Heart Boot Camp led by John Eldredge and his team delivered through video sessions. It's online. It's free. Go to wildatheart.org to see if a BASIC is being offered at a location near you. Or better yet, consider hosting a BASIC for a small group of like-minded men.

The next section offers a curated menu of the different content and studies that Wild at Heart Ministries recommends. Continuing into another year together can be as easy as picking what content is speaking to your group and working through it next.

If your year together has come to a close and the season of living life together with this particular group of men is over, that is perfectly appropriate.

We are meant to live life in seasons, and that is true for relationships as well.

But having gone through this material, you are equipped to lead other men into the deep waters of the masculine journey. Consider finding men who need this and leading them through it. That may be your next adventure.

Above all, continue walking with God and stay connected with like-hearted men. Doing so will lead you into the next chapter of an epic story.

ADDITIONAL GROUP STUDY OPTIONS

We've created this final section as a resource for additional content for your group.

You can use it if you've finished your first year and are looking for what to do next—either on your own or together.

It is also for current groups that have fewer than eight men and need extra material for your year.

Each resource listed is available in book, video series, and study guide formats.

All Things New (John Eldredge)

What will be the great sustaining hope of your life?

More than anything else, how you envision your future shapes your current experience. If you knew that God was going to restore your life and everything you love any day now, if you believed a great and glorious goodness was coming to you—not in heaven but right here on this earth—you would have a hope to see you through anything, an anchor for your soul, "an unbreakable spiritual lifeline, reaching past all appearances right to the very presence of God" (Heb. 6:19 MSG).

Most Christians fail to look forward to their future because their views of heaven are vague, religious, and, frankly, boring. Hope begins when we understand that for the believer *nothing is lost*. Heaven is not a life in the clouds; it is not endless harp strumming or worship singing.

Rather, the life we long for, the paradise that Adam and Eve knew, is precisely the life that is coming to us. And that life is coming soon.

Get Your Life Back (John Eldredge)

If you are truly honest with yourself, are you happy most of the time? Do you feel deeply loved? Are you excited about your future? How often do you feel lighthearted? If your honest answer to these questions is not optimistic, you are not alone.

Our souls are deeply entangled in this maddening and broken world. *Get Your Life Back* offers profoundly simple practices, or graces, to help you recover your soul, not in a cosmic, abstract future, but every day, right now, right here.

You do not need to abandon your life to get it back, but retake it through the one-minute pause, benevolent detachment, everyday beauty, and other life-changing graces.

Moving Mountains (John Eldredge)

How would it feel to enter into prayer with confidence and assurance—certain that God heard you and that your prayers would make a difference?

It would likely feel amazing and unfamiliar. That's because often our prayers seem to be met with silence or don't appear to change anything. Either response can lead to disappointment or even despair in the face of our ongoing battles and unmet longings—especially when we don't know if we're doing something wrong or if some prayers just don't work.

Moving Mountains shows you how to experience the power of daily prayer, learn the major types of prayers—including those of intervention, consecration, warfare, and healing—and discover the intimacy of the cry of the heart prayer, listening prayer, and praying Scripture.

This is your invitation to engage in the kind of prayers that can move God's heart as well as the mountains before you.

Walking with God (John Eldredge)

Our deepest need is to live in conversation with God. To hear his voice. To follow him intimately. This is the single most life-changing habit that a human being can adopt because it brings us back to the source of life.

Yet most Christians have never been taught how to have a conversation with the Creator. God created us for intimate fellowship with himself, and in doing so he established the goal of our existence— to know him, love him, and live our lives in an intimate relationship with him.

In *Walking with God*, John Eldredge takes you on a year-long expedition in search of true conversational intimacy with God. It's your invitation to recapture this lost treasure of Christian spirituality— learning to hear the voice of God.

John Eldredge is a bestselling author and counselor. He is also president of Wild at Heart, a ministry devoted to helping people discover the heart of God and recover their own hearts in God's love. John and his wife, Stasi, live near Colorado Springs, Colorado.

Luke Eldredge, a Colorado native, is finishing an MFA in poetry at Colorado State University. He received his Bachelor's degree in Literature from Whitworth University. He has been writing articles for And Sons Magazine since 2013. Luke is passionate about the power of poetry and exploring the Colorado mountains, and is currently finishing work on his first book of poems. Luke lives with his wife, Olivia, and their dog, Rainier.

Acknowledgments

Special thanks to the following for their essential role in making this project a reality: Darren Thornberry, Karen Christakis, Wookie Jones, Lorie DeWorken, Alex Burton, Jon Dale, Nic Bovee, Stacey Burton, and Allen Arnold.

LOOKING FOR MORE?
Visit **WildatHeart.org**
for a wealth of additional
resources including film series,
podcasts, and prayers.